Richard Lang first saw who he really was in 1970, in a workshop with Douglas Harding, author of *On Having No Head*. Since then he has continued exploring and sharing this direct way of awakening, leading hundreds of workshops around the world. Richard is co-ordinator of The Shollond Trust, a UK charity founded to share the philosophy and practical awareness exercises – the experiments - of Douglas Harding. Richard's aim is to share the experience and meaning of who we really are as widely as possible.

Seeing
who you really
are

A Modern Guide to Your True Identity

Richard Lang

including extracts from the writings of

Douglas Harding

Published by The Shollond Trust,
87B Cazenove Road,
London N16 6BB.
headexchange@gn.apc.org
www.headless.org

The Shollond Trust is a UK charity reg. no 1059551.

Copyright ©Richard Lang 2012.

First published in 2003 by Watkins Publishing.

Design by Rangs Graphics & Design
www.rangsgraphics.com

ISBN 978-0-9554512-6-3

The Shollond Trust

For David

ACKNOWLEDGEMENTS

My thanks to Douglas Harding: for tirelessly working to share this precious vision; for his articles and the interviews I conducted with him; and for the many quotations from various spiritual traditions.

I am also grateful to Bryan Nuttall for his illustrations; to the friends whose articles, emails and poetry I have included; and to René for inviting me, years ago now, to give an online course – from which this book grew.

My thanks also to Danielle Bol de Greve for typing the text.

Colin Oliver's poems are from *Stepping into Brilliant Air*.

CONTENTS

FOREWORD

I first met Richard Lang in 1970 at a Buddhist summer school in Hertfordshire. He saw immediately the truth of the Insight I sought to share with everyone there. Richard was then seventeen years old, on the point of leaving school and going up to Cambridge to read history - an ideal time to see into one's essential Nature (I, alas, left it till I was thirty-three). What a kick-start to one's adulthood!

Richard is now fifty. I have stayed in touch with him ever since that summer school, and I can testify that all the while I have known him he has devoted his time and energies to the twofold purpose of practising the vision of his true and divine Nature until it becomes effortless and virtually automatic and sharing that vision with all who show interest.

The sharing of this vision, for Richard as for me, is by no means an intellectual or conceptual ploy, but on the contrary is a perceptual or sensory experience. That is why his endeavour to share his vision with all and sundry takes the form of experiments or exercises in actually seeing what one sees, instead of what one fancies one sees or is told one sees. And that is why, in this book, he insists that you, his reader, actually do the experiments he describes and not just read about them, which is no good at all. Like me, Richard believes that one fine day an influential though not necessarily large section of the population will recognize that this vision of our divine Nature is the mark of true maturity, and the only hope for the suffering world.

What's more, we are both sure that every human who says: 'I AM this or that or whatever' - which, as Meister Eckhart points out, only God can really, really say - is a unique and quite indispensable aspect of His infinite variety.

Shankara, the great Hindu sage and philosopher, tells us, 'This being-the-Self-of-all is the highest state of consciousness of the Self, His supreme natural state. But when, before this, one feels oneself to be other than the Self of all, even by a hair's breadth, that state is delusion.'

D. E. Harding
February 2003

PREFACE

In the winter of 1998 I found a website where you could teach free courses on spirituality over the internet. The website would advertise the course and anyone visiting could sign up. Running a course involved sending out emails to the enrolled students, who could then respond either to the teacher or to anyone present in the chat room (set up for the occasion).

I decided on nine lessons, sending out one a day, and called the course 'Seeing Who You Really Are'. With nearly thirty years' experience of Seeing I felt confident enough to leave the writing until the course began. I wanted to write for a live audience, to feel my way as I went along, adapting my teaching as I received feedback from participants. If people weren't getting the point of who they really were, or were finding problems with it, then I could address these issues as the course developed.

The first time I taught this course about five hundred people signed up. The second time, eighteen months later, nine hundred enrolled.

Writing a lesson each day for nine days was demanding (I was also working during this time). I remember finishing the fourth lesson, emailing it out late at night, and then realizing I needed to start writing the next one if I was going to have it ready in time. But at this point, with only four lessons completed and five more to go, I didn't know what to write. I visited the chat room and exchanged ideas with friends there who were following the course, but didn't come away with anything I could use. Just wishes of good luck (and the feeling, 'Rather, you, Richard, than me!'). I took a bath (it was well after midnight by then) and as I soaked in the hot water I was feeling concerned. Five hundred people waiting for the next lesson and I'd no idea what to write…

As I lay in the bath I finally accepted I didn't know what to do. I let go and relaxed back into who I really was - this wise emptiness, this mysterious yet audible silence. I realised it was now up to my deepest self, this fertile blankness, to produce something - and soon. This course was now in its hands. Until that moment I had been resisting letting go, trying to figure things out by myself. Now it was clear I couldn't manage on my own. There was no alternative but to surrender to the One within me. This, after all, is what Seeing is about - awakening to one's deepest being and surrendering to its guidance.

For a while my mind was blank, but then an idea came to me - write about resistance and surrender. So that's what I did. From first-hand experience! From then on I found that each day I had enough ideas for that day's lesson. The One had yet again come up with what was needed.

The eight chapters in Part I, 'A Course in Seeing', are developed versions of those nine lessons, with the last two merged into one. I have included feedback from participants (some of whose names I have lost) and articles by Douglas Harding, pioneer of this way of Seeing. These articles were part of the original classes, as was much of the feedback from participants.

Part II - articles, email correspondence from Seeing friends, and interviews - shows how easy it is to See. It is an encouraging fact that there are now growing numbers of people awakening to who they really are. I hope this book helps this awakening spread even more widely. Perhaps in the not-too-distant future it will be normal to be conscious of one's true nature. I hope so. Overlooking who we really are leads to confrontation and suffering.

This book invites you to see who you really are. Through its practical awareness exercises – the experiments - it shows you how. If through reading this book (and doing the experiments) you awaken to who you really are – and I believe you will, for there is nothing simpler than seeing your true self - then this Vision will have taken another step towards being accepted as natural and normal in society. And once you are seeing who you really are, you are qualified to share this awareness with others. I hope you do.

Read this book, do the experiments and step through a doorway into the endless wonders of who you really are.

What have you got to lose by seeing who you really are? Nothing but an illusion!

What have you got to gain? Everything.

R.L. 2003

PREFACE TO THE SECOND EDITION

With this second edition comes the opportunity to revise. It has been a pleasure to read through my book and change things here and there, making the expression clearer wherever I can. I have also added insights that have grown in me since this book was first published. Of course, this clear, bright, full emptiness hasn't grown at all. It's exactly the same now as it was eight years ago when this book was first published. Exactly the same as it's always been. Bless it for being so reliable!

R.L. 2011

PART I

A Course in Seeing

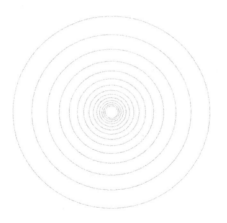

CHAPTER ONE

OVERVIEW

This is a step-by-step guide to *seeing* who we really are, the one Self in all beings.

As well as seeing the One, we will also be exploring the implications of living consciously as the One. This Seeing path was developed by the English philosopher Douglas Harding. It is a contemporary Western path to Self-Realisation that dovetails with both modern science and traditional mysticism. Douglas Harding, born in 1909, first saw who he really was in 1943 in India. Subsequently he wrote *The Hierarchy of Heaven and Earth – A New Diagram of Man in the Universe*. This is a truly great book of philosophy. It was published in 1952 with a preface by C. S. Lewis who described it as 'a work of the highest genius' – Lewis said that reading it had made him 'roaring drunk'! Harding followed *The Hierarchy* in 1961 with his better-known book *On Having No Head*. Then in the late '60s and early '70s Harding invented his *experiments*. These test the central message of his philosophy, his hypothesis that 'you are not what you look like'. During the last forty years of his life, as well as continuing to write, Harding travelled widely giving workshops, sharing the experience of 'who we really are' with many people. He died in 2007 aged 97.

In 1970 I attended a workshop with Harding. After posing the question 'Who are we really?', Harding introduced his experiments. I was astonished. They worked. I saw who I really was - my true Self became clearly and brilliantly visible. Inspired by the effectiveness of the experiments I became involved in the work of sharing this Way as widely as possible.

THE HYPOTHESIS

Who are you really? What are you *at no distance* from yourself? Our hypothesis claims that *you are not what you look like*. In other words, though you appear to others (at a distance) as a unique person, to yourself (at no distance), you are boundless and timeless *emptiness – awake space* that is *capacity* for the world.

This hypothesis can also be expressed in spiritual language: At your centre is God, Buddha-nature, the Tao, the Self – we give this Reality many names. Closer to you than your hands and feet and nearer to you than your breathing is the One, the Source and Container of all things. When you see this One, and live consciously as this Reality, you find peace and freedom, beauty and love, inspiration and guidance.

You don't have to believe this hypothesis. Throughout this book you will be testing it. You will always be encouraged to rely on your own experience rather than someone else's, to test the truth of any claims about you by seeing for yourself what you are. There's a simple reason for this: you are the only one that is right where you are, so only you are in a position to say what you are at centre. No matter how clever or revered another person might be, they are not at your centre and therefore do not have the authority to say what you are there.

Clearly our hypothesis about who you really are is extraordinary. What could be more amazing than asserting that at the heart of all your appearances you are the one Self within all beings, the timeless source of everything, the Self-Originating One? If it's true it should make the hair stand up on the back of your neck. Surely it's worth spending a few moments to see if it's true. And if it is true, then surely it's worth finding out what benefits and blessings flow from being aware of, from consciously being the Self - the self-originating, all-powerful, all-knowing, omnipresent, infinitely loving and merciful Self. Of course, it's up to each of us. We don't have to look! Nor do we have to value the Self when we see it!

People who do the *experiments* and see who they really are, say you don't need to change anything to see the One. In other words, this is seeing who you are now, just as you are. You don't have to become more spiritual or clever, or different in any way to see and be your true Self. No matter what your personality or situation, no matter what you have done or not done, you need only be willing to take a fresh look at yourself, need only be willing to look at the place you are looking out of. (And be willing to continue looking.) When you look, you see the treasure at the heart of your being – the treasure that *is* your being, available now and free. Then, in their own time, many good things flow from this Seeing - gifts that are special and unique to you.

GUIDELINES

In his *Toolkit for Testing the Incredible Hypothesis,* Douglas Harding offered guidelines for seeing who you really are. These guidelines correspond with what mystics say about awakening to our true Self:

1. What to look for: no-thing, having no qualities, transparent like air or water, boundless, changeless, empty.

2. Where to look: right where you are, at the Looker.

3. How to look: trustingly like a child, and as if for the first time. Go by what you can see for yourself, not by what you think or have been told. Remember that only you are in a position to see how it is where you are. You are the sole authority on what it's like being you.

4. Who to look for: a truly superhuman Being, with powers to match and fully Self-aware.

APPEARANCE, REALITY AND RELATIVITY

Harding's experiments guide your attention inwards to your central reality. But first, before looking at your central reality, consider what you are for others: *what you look like.*

What anything is depends partly on the range of the observer. Look at something nearby - a chair, for example. At this distance it has a particular shape and colour, but get closer to it (with the aid of a powerful microscope) and it changes. It becomes fibres. Closer still (using more powerful instruments), it becomes molecules, atoms, electrons and so on, till there's almost nothing left to observe. Like an onion it has layers - layers you peel as you approach. It remains recognisable as a chair only when you keep your distance.

You have layers too. At several metres you are a person. But if I move closer you become just a head, then a patch of skin. If I could move even closer (using various instruments) I would pass through your cellular, molecular and atomic layers, peeling away your appearances till there's hardly anything left of you.

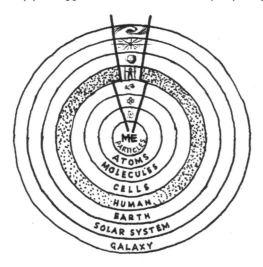

Illustration by Douglas Harding

On the other hand, if I move away, your body becomes absorbed into the surrounding environment: your local town or city which in turn is absorbed by your country and continent. Zooming away still further, I pass through your planetary, solar and galactic layers. These layers are also you - you at great distances - though you may not usually think of them as your 'self'. But though you may not identify with them, you depend on your distant layers just as much as you depend on your near ones. Your sun, for example, is as vital to you as your heart.

What is at the centre of all your layers? What is the reality behind all your appearances? The nearer I approach, the less I find. At very close range you are almost nothing. However, no matter how close I get, I fail to peel away a final layer, if there is one, and see into your centre. I am unable to unmask you, unable to uncover your underlying identity, the reality at your centre. The heart of you remains an inaccessible mystery to me.

Fortunately there is someone who can see the mystery at your centre, the reality behind all your appearances. Who is that?

You!

You can see your central reality because you are there. You, and you alone, are perfectly placed to see what you are at centre.

LOOKING FOR YOURSELF

How can you see what you are at centre? It's simple and easy. Here is the first experiment that guides your attention to the core of yourself.

— EXPERIMENT 1 —

Pointing at your Centre

Point at something nearby and look at it. (Actually point and look!) From this distance you see a *thing* there. Notice its form and colour.

Point at your shoe. Another thing. Notice its form and colour.

Point at your torso. Yet another thing. Notice its form and colour.

Now you come to the most important part: turning your attention round 180 degrees and looking back at the place you are looking out of. Point back at the place where others see your face. (Actually do this.) You are now pointing at the one place in the world that is no distance from you. What do you see?

Are you pointing at another *thing* now? Do you see any shape or colour there? Do you see your face? Put aside what you *think* or *assume* is there, put aside what you have *learned* is there, and *look*.

Only you are in a position to see what you are at centre since you alone are your side of your pointing finger. Don't rely on what others say is there, rely on your own experience.

Here is my experience: *there* I see my pointing finger with the room beyond it, but *here* where I'm pointing I see nothing. Here I see no colours, no shapes, no face.

Instead of seeing my face here, I see space, transparency, clarity, emptiness. I am this aware space, this awake emptiness.

At the same time as seeing this emptiness, I see my finger and the scene beyond – the space here is full of the world, including sensations, thoughts and sounds. Though verbally I distinguish between this awake emptiness and the things it contains, I find no boundary between them: the space here merges with and becomes the world. I am both this space *and* all that is in it.

Keep pointing at, and looking at, the place you are looking out of, the place where others see your face. Be curious. Don't assume you know what and who you are and therefore don't need to look. You have been taught that right where you are, at zero distance, you are a *something*, a person. Are you? Don't let others talk you out of what you *see*. Be your own authority. Are you what you look like? Are you a person at centre or are you capacity for the world?

REFLECTION

You are now seeing who you really are. 'But I see nothing!' you may object. Yes, I see nothing too, but this is a special *nothing* because it's aware of itself as *nothing*. (You know it's aware because you are this nothing and self-evidently you are aware. You are not an unconscious, unseeing space but a seeing space, alive to yourself.)

As well as being aware of your nothingness, you are also aware of all that your nothingness contains, from your pointing finger to the stars in the night sky. You are this seeing space and all you see.

Perhaps you are thinking that you cannot be seeing your true Self because what we are doing is so simple and easy. It's too simple and easy – there's nothing to it! Can it really be this simple? Well, it is, thank goodness. And as well as being simple, it's also not necessarily dramatic, not necessarily a 'wow' experience. Seeing who we really are is simply seeing what is given – or not given. It is looking into what is true rather than trying to generate special experiences of 'oneness', for example, or 'ego-loss', or 'union with God'. Mystical experiences are interesting and exciting and certainly have their place, but they are not essential to seeing who we really are. And attractive as mystical experiences are, the danger is that we become so interested in them that we are diverted from the plain experience of seeing our true Self. (The paradox is that when we put awareness of our true Self first rather than chasing mystical experiences, all the mystical experiences we need come to us, in their own time and way.)

If you still think you haven't 'got it', then please be patient. Perhaps another experiment will mean more to you than the pointing experiment.

Over the centuries many people from different religions and cultures have seen and valued who they really are. Here are some of their reflections about the wonderful treasure they found. Their words will, I hope, encourage us to value this treasure.

You are like a mirage in the desert which the thirsty man thinks is water; but when he comes up to it he finds it is nothing. And where he thought it was, there he finds God. Similarly, if you were to examine yourself, you would find it to be nothing, and instead you would find God. That is to say, you would find God instead of yourself, and there would be nothing left of you but a name without a form.

AL-ALAWI

~~~~~

When all things are reduced to naught in you then you shall see God.

MEISTER ECKHART

~~~~~

In this kind of seeing, one only sees that no shape is there.

THE SECRET OF THE GOLDEN FLOWER

~~~~~~

All that has form, sound, colour, may be classed under the head 'thing'… But a man can attain to formlessness and vanquish death. And with that which is in possession of the eternal, how can mere things compare?

CHUANG-TZU

~~~~~~

It is a great joy to realise that the Fundamental Nature is qualityless.

GAMPOPA

~~~~~~

He that beholds his own Face - his light is greater than the light of creatures. Though he die, his sight is everlasting, because his sight is the sight of the Creator.

RUMI

~~~~~~

I'm looking for the face I had
Before the world was made.

W. B. YEATS

~~~~~~

Loosing and dropping off body and mind, your Original Face is clear before you.

ZAZEN-GI

~~~~~~

Not one of the 1700 koans of Zen has any other purpose than to make us see our Original Face.

DAITO KOKUSHI

~~~~~~

Here is a letter I received from an American friend who is the abbot of a Zen temple in Japan:

Dear Richard,

Something interesting happened last night. I was visited by a man that I didn't know very well and he noticed a calligraphic scroll I had hanging, with only the character for 'Mu' (nothingess) on it. He asked, 'Toler san, have you ever entered the world of Mu?' I said, 'Yes, many times.' Then he asked, 'How can you do it? At what times do you do it?' I said, 'Oh, you can do it anytime.'

He asked, 'How?' So I led him through the pointing exercise. When I came to the question, 'Now, what do you see at the place where your finger is pointing?' he said, 'Nothing.' I said, 'Well, that's Mu, isn't it?' He thought about that for about ten seconds, then suddenly laughed loudly and clapped his hands and said, 'I've been pondering that for years, and you showed me in a minute!' and thanked me profusely.

Warmest regards,

John

FURTHER REFLECTIONS

For others we are things in the world. What kind of thing we are depends on how far others are from us. At medium range we are human. We are very familiar with this view of ourselves. In fact, we are so familiar with it that much of the time we live as if it's the *only* view of ourselves. In assuming this is our identity, we overlook the very different views of ourselves from other distances, and in particular from no distance. The pointing experiment reveals what we are at no distance.

However, it's all too easy to glimpse our true Self for a moment, here at no distance, and then drift away from it. Before we know it we are again overlooking who we really are, forgetting to See. Our aim in this course is to keep bringing our attention back to the place we are looking out of. This is a meditation for each moment.

What difference might conscious facelessness make in our lives if we take it seriously and attend to it?

As a person I am separate from others, I have limited resources, I am mortal. These are facts of life and must be accepted. But if this is the only way I see myself - the way I appear to others - then it's not surprising if I feel alienated, lonely, poor, frustrated and frightened. However, when I see who I really am, a different view of myself opens up: my own view of myself. As *capacity* no one is outside me: I am not separate from others but include everyone within my being. Ongoing awareness of this gradually but deeply affects the way I relate to 'others', for I see that my neighbour is my Self. Indeed, all beings are my Self. This is the end of loneliness and the source of unconditional love. Awareness that my true Self is unlimited, the inexhaustible source from which all things flow, means I am infinitely wealthy, richer than all the millionaires in the world put together. Recognising this gradually reduces my greed. And, conscious of my divine identity, I realise that since all flows from my true Self, all that happens is my will. Therefore nothing frustrates or frightens me. Even death has no power over the One we all are.

At the same time I continue being aware that I am a vulnerable human being – I remain self-conscious. In other words, I live a two-sided life: looking both inwards and outwards, I am both divine and human. On the one hand as a person I am completely dependent on my divine Self – it is the being of my being, the source from which my life flows. I couldn't exist for a moment without its life-giving Presence. On the other hand, without my humanity my divine Self could not express itself: the All-Powerful, All-Loving One needs our legs to get about, our hands to do things, our voices to communicate, our hearts to feel.

These are initial reflections about Seeing. However, one glimpse of our true Self won't make much difference. If we want to receive the blessings our true Self will shower upon us, we need to keep bringing our attention back to it, back to the place we are looking out of, back to this seeing space, back to this full emptiness.

Of course, don't believe these claims. Test them for yourself.

In the following extract Douglas Harding describes the moment he first saw who he really was.

The True Seeing

Douglas Harding, from *On Having No Head*

The best day of my life - my rebirthday, so to speak - was when I found I had no head. This is not a literary gambit, a witticism designed to arouse interest at any cost. I mean it in all seriousness: I have no head.

It was eighteen years ago, when I was thirty-three, that I made the discovery. Though it certainly came out of the blue, it did so in response to an urgent enquiry; I had for several months been absorbed in the question: what am I? The fact that I happened to be walking in the Himalayas at the time probably had little to do with it; though in that country unusual states of mind are said to come more easily. However that may be, a very still clear day, and a view from the ridge where I stood, over misty blue valleys to the highest mountain range in the world, with Kangchenjunga and Everest unprominent among its snow-peaks, made a setting worthy of the grandest vision.

What actually happened was something absurdly simple and unspectacular: I stopped thinking. A peculiar quiet, an odd kind of alert limpness or numbness, came over me. Reason and imagination and all mental chatter died down. For once, words really failed me. Past and future dropped away. I forgot who and what I was, my name, manhood, animalhood, all that could be called mine. It was as if I had been born that instant, brand-new, mindless, innocent of all memories. There existed only the Now, that present moment and what was clearly given in it. To look was enough. And what I found was khaki trouserlegs terminating downwards in a pair of brown shoes, khaki sleeves terminating sideways in a pair of pink hands, and a khaki shirtfront terminating upwards in - absolutely nothing whatsoever! Certainly not in a head.

It took me no time at all to notice that this nothing, this hole where a head should have been was no ordinary vacancy, no mere nothing. On the contrary, it was very much occupied. It was a vast emptiness vastly filled, a nothing that found room for everything - room for grass, trees, shadowy distant hills, and far above them snowpeaks like a row of angular clouds riding the blue sky. I had lost a head and gained a world.

It was all, quite literally, breathtaking. I seemed to stop breathing altogether, absorbed in the Given. Here it was, this superb scene, brightly shining in the clear air, alone and unsupported, mysteriously suspended in the void, and (and this was the real miracle, the wonder and delight) utterly free of 'me', unstained by any observer. Its total presence was my total absence, body and soul. Lighter than air, cleared than glass, altogether released from myself, I was nowhere around.

Yet in spite of the magical and uncanny quality of this vision, it was no dream, no esoteric revelation. Quite the reverse: it felt like a sudden waking from the sleep of ordinary life, an end to dreaming. It was self-luminous reality for once swept clean of all obscuring mind. It was the revelation, at long last, of the perfectly obvious. It was a lucid moment in a confused life history. It was a ceasing to ignore something which (since early childhood at any rate) I had always been too busy or too clever to see. It was naked, uncritical attention to what had all along been staring me in the face - my utter facelessness. In short, it was all perfectly simple and plain and straightforward, beyond argument, thought, and words. There arose no questions, no reference beyond the experience itself, but only peace and a quiet joy, and the sensation of having dropped an intolerable burden.

Don't we dream of discovering something wonderful, a shining treasure, something magical and marvellous, something so fresh and endless it will inspire and rejuvenate us again and again? Here is just such a treasure.

It is also a highly practical tool. In possession of it - or when it's in possession of us - we have a tool that works perfectly in any situation and with any problem. It's right for any job.

We will now do more experiments. The experiments guide us to who we really are. They invite us to *look*, simply and directly, at the place we are looking out of. *Thinking* about who we are, important as it is, is not the same as *seeing* who we are. The main thing is *Seeing*. (We will be exploring the other senses too). Anyway, since it's possible to see who we really are, why settle for just thinking about it?

— EXPERIMENT 2 —

Your Headless Body

Look at your body. You see your legs, arms and torso. You see your nose: a large, shadowy thing on the left or right side of your field of vision. But do you see the rest of your head? Isn't your body headless?

Mine is! When I look above my shoulders I discover nothing but space for the world. My head is nowhere to be found.

With your finger trace the line above your chest where your body fades out. Here is the edge of your world! Above this line is nothing! Nothing but the world! Imagining my head here, I overlook what I really am.

If you are going somewhere it's sensible to have an idea of your destination before setting out so you will recognise it when you arrive. Then you begin your journey, travelling from *here* to *there*. It's the same with travelling to your true Self. What does your true Self look like? Those who are aware of it say it's a clear, boundless, awake space full of the world, and it's nearer than near. Knowing this, you set off – except your journey is not from *here* to *there*, but from *there* to *here*. Start by placing your finger *there* on your knee. Then move it to your tummy, then to your chest, and then keep going in the same direction till it disappears. Look at the place it has vanished into. This place is *here*. Is it clear, boundless, awake, and full of the world? If it is, then you have reached your destination. Congratulations!

———————————

The precious Vajra sword is right here and its purpose is to cut off the head.

TAI-HUI

~~~~~~~~~

How wonderful is the path of love, when the headless one is exalted.

HAFIZ

~~~~~~~~~

This travelling hat may look small, but when I put it on it covers the whole cosmos.

HUANG-PO

~~~~~~~~~

That head of clay is from the earth, and this pure Head from Heaven.

RUMI

— EXPERIMENT 3 —

The Single Eye

How many eyes are you looking out of? Other people see *two* when they look at you, and you see two in the mirror, but how many are you looking out of *from your point of view?* Take a fresh look in case you are overlooking something both obvious and wonderful.

I am looking out of *one* eye. In fact, it's not even an *eye* - it's an undivided, edgeless space, a single, frameless Window that's always open.

To bring your attention to your single Eye, hold your hands out in front of you as if they are a pair of glasses you are going to put on.

You see *two* holes.

Bring them towards you and put them on.

What has happened to the dividing line between the two holes? Hasn't it disappeared, leaving one undivided space you are looking out of?

Observe the edge of your field of vision. Can you look at it directly? I can't. Is there a clear line around it, a definite edge? I find the world fades out gradually. Into what? I see nothing beyond the edge of the world – nothing except my eternally open Eye. This Eye goes on and on forever, in every direction. All things are within it.

From this clear Window I see my hands and desk; looking further I see my garden. My view from this Window is unique to me – no one else sees exactly what I see. But how could my view inwards, into this Clarity, be different from what anyone else sees when they look within? There's nothing here to see differently.

My view out from this Window is always changing. This week the first daffodils are flowering in my garden - Winter is giving way to Spring. But the view in isn't changing: there's nothing here to change.

You can see your single Eye anywhere, anytime. Discover how relaxing it is – being this clear, edgeless Window.

He became one-eyed.

ATTAR

~~~~~~~~~

When your eye is single, your whole body shall be full of light, having no place dark.

JESUS

~~~~~~~~~

The Tathagata became the Eye of the universe.

PARINIRVANA SUTRA

~~~~~~~~~

Real vision is eyeless.

ANANDAMAYIMA

~~~~~~~~~

I look and listen without using eyes and ears.

LIEH-TZU

~~~~~~~~~

If there were no eye, what? If there were no ear, what? If there were no mouth, what? If there were no mind, what? If one has to face such circumstances and knows how to act then one is in the company of the ancient Patriarchs and Buddhas. Anyone in that company is satisfied.

BLUE CLIFF RECORDS

~~~~~~~~~

I become a transparent eyeball; I am nothing; I see all.

RALPH WALDO EMERSON

DOUBTS AND QUESTIONS

We have begun our enquiry. You may find yourself having doubts: 'But I can see my face in the mirror! I can touch my head! This is all too visual: what happens when I close my eyes? How would you share this with a blind person? What about my mind: where are my thoughts if I don't have a head?' In other words, you're questioning whether this book's hypothesis is true when investigated from every angle. Great! That's the spirit. Doubt what you are told. Test things for yourself. As we progress through this book, we will continue testing our hypothesis every way we can.

As well as questions about the validity of Seeing, there are questions about its usefulness: 'What's the point of this? What difference will Seeing make in my life? Yes, I see no face here, but so what?'

The best answers to these questions are our own. Perhaps when we are with others we discover that Seeing means we are less anxiously self-conscious, or not anxious at all. This is a valuable discovery. Or in a stressful situation we realize that at centre we are stress-free. What a resource! Perhaps when we feel trapped in a problem and see no way out, we put our trust in this mysterious source and discover, to our relief, that it takes care of us, though perhaps not in the way we want or expect. Such experiences convince us of the value of Seeing. On the other hand, if we don't test it, if we don't give it a chance, we won't realise how valuable it is. It will then be nothing more than an interesting idea.

HOMEWORK

- Point to your facelessness several times during the day and attend to what is given (or not given).
- Notice that you are looking out of a single Eye. Keep noticing this Window, whenever you remember.
- Sit for five minutes each day, eyes open, with the sole purpose of Seeing.

CHAPTER TWO

REVIEW

Who are you? It depends on the distance of your observer. From a few metres, more or less, you are human; at closer ranges you are cells, molecules, particles; from further away you are a planet, a star, a galaxy. In other words you have layers like an onion. What are you at zero distance, right in the centre of all your layers? Only you are in a position to say for only you are there. The experiments guide your attention to your centre, to the place you are looking out of. Are you what you look like? Do you see an appearance there or capacity for the world? Are you a thing or room for things? Don't ask others: look for yourself. I am room for things! Looking in, I find nothing at all: pure capacity. But, wonder of wonders, looking out from this absolute poverty, I am wealthy beyond my wildest dreams - all things are within me, all the way from my headless body to the stars – to *my* stars!

In Chapter One I quoted several mystics, not appealing to them as authorities to follow blindly but as sources of inspiration. (Instead of trying to fit our experience to their descriptions, let's test their descriptions by our experience!) Here is more from these wise ones, these seers who were awake to and valued who they really were.

Jesus said: A man who looks on himself only from outside, and not also from inside, makes himself small.

GOSPEL of MANI

~~~~~~~~~

It is easier to see the Self than to see a gooseberry in the palm of your hand.

RAMANA MAHARSHI

~~~~~~~~~

Who is it that repeats the Buddha's name? We should try to find out where this who comes from and what it looks like.

HSU-YUN

~~~~~~~~~

– EXPERIMENT 4 –

The Mirror

'But what about the mirror? I can see my face there.' Let's investigate this.

When you look in a mirror you see not only *what* your face looks like but also *where* it is – it's *there* in the mirror, not *here* above your chest. Find a mirror and see *where* your face is – it's about a metre away!

Is there a second face on your side of the mirror?

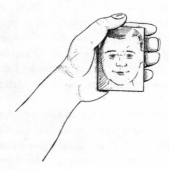

When I look in a mirror I see my face there but I find no face on my side of the glass. Here I am free of my face. I am not what I look like. I am capacity *here* for my appearance *there*. Are you the same?

If you bring the mirror towards you, you see different images. These are still reflections of you, though the mirror contains less of your face: first you see all your face, then just an eye, finally a blur…

If you could bring the mirror closer it would reveal even closer layers: cells, molecules, atoms…

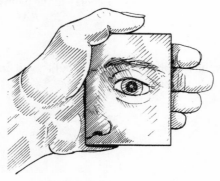

Obviously you cannot do this. But not only does the mirror fail to reveal these closer layers, it fails to show you what you are *at centre* since you cannot place it there. The mirror is good for showing you who you are at arm's length, but hopeless for showing you who you are at zero distance. It reveals your regional appearances but not your central reality.

Look in a full-length mirror placed a few metres away. Now your whole body is on show, out there at the range where it belongs. It manifests *there* (not *here*). If others want to see your whole body, from head to toes, then they must look at you from roughly the same distance as that mirror – much closer and you grow so big that parts of you vanish, or much further away and you grow so small that you disappear into your environment. In other words, there's a zone around you where you appear human, both to others and to yourself in the mirror.

Imagine placing mirrors at greater distances. First, picture a huge mirror in the sky. You would still see your appearance there, but the image would no longer be of a person. Depending on where you live you might see England, France, the USA, China… You are looking at your *national* face.

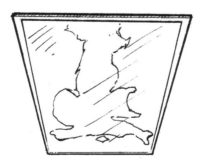

Now imagine a mirror on the moon. There's your beautiful *planetary* face.

Imagine a mirror on Proxima Centauri (our nearest star), wait 4.2 years for the image to reach you, and discover what you are at that distance. If you haven't guessed, you're a star!

Finally, imagine a mirror on Andromeda (a neighbouring galaxy), wait about 3 million years for the image to reach you, and see what you are at that distance. Amazingly, you are a vast, glittering spiral galaxy, billions of years old.

What an astonishing, many-levelled body you have! And you thought you were only human!

THE FACE GAME

Let's return to the more familiar human level. What do I normally do when I see my face in the mirror? I play tricks with it.

As well as *looking at it*, I imagine I'm *looking out of it*. I've never seen my face on my side of the mirror, but I believe it's here (because society says so).

To maintain this belief, here in more detail are the games I play with my face in the mirror.

Putting on my Mirror Face

I pretend to reach into the mirror, grab hold of my face and pull it out.

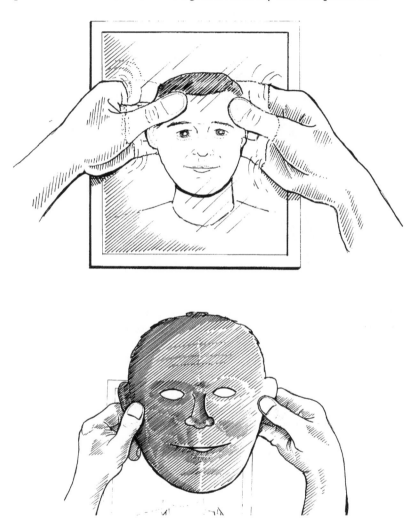

Then I imagine flipping it inside out like a rubber mask so that it's facing the other way.

It's small, so with my imagination I stretch it to make it bigger. (Measure the face in the mirror between your thumb and forefinger and see how small it is.)

Now I move this imaginary, inside out, enlarged face towards the place I'm looking out of and imagine attaching it here to nothing. I pretend to put it on like a mask. As I do this I imagine changing it from being hard, flat, smooth and cool (behind the glass *there*) to being soft, uneven, rough in places and warm *here*. (I marry the visible image there to the invisible sensations here.)

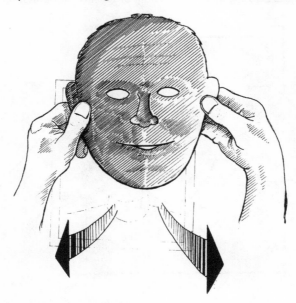

Then I live and act *as if* that face is *here*. Without realizing it, I'm playing a game of pretence: *the face game* - the game of having a face *here*. Almost everyone plays this game - everyone except babies, some unsocialised people and seers. Without questioning it, we accept that we are what we look like, that we are *here* what we see in the mirror *there*.

Leaving my Face in the Mirror

Looking in the mirror *honestly* shows me not only *what* my face looks like but also *where* it is – it's there in the mirror. When I'm seeing that my face is there, not here, I'm not playing tricks with it. I'm not stealing it from the mirror, not imagining it inside out and all the rest. I'm letting it be *what* it is, *where* it is.

Being faceless is a profound relief. Instead of playing *the face game* – instead of performing all those tiresome tricks, day in, day out - you simply are what you are. Whether or not you are in front of a mirror, you see there's no image at your centre. There's nothing here to think about, to keep going, to remember or worry about, nothing here that you have to be sure of or have to prove to others, nothing here that separates you from others, nothing here that will age or die. Consciously being your real Self, you are free and at peace.

At the same time you remain aware of what you look like. You are both human and divine.

…man, proud man,
Drest in a little brief authority,
Most ignorant of what he's most assured,
His glassy essence, like an angry ape,
Plays such fantastic tricks before high heaven
As make the angels weep;

SHAKESPEARE

~~~~~~~~~~~~

A young friend in a workshop - a boy of eight or nine - looked in the mirror and said: 'The mirror is like a magnet - it pulls all this stuff here out there.'

DOUGLAS HARDING

~~~~~~~~~~~~

A friend's daughter, aged four, was told to go and wash her face. She went to the bathroom and started washing her face - in the mirror…

DOUGLAS HARDING

~~~~~~~~~~~~

Estelle: 'I feel so queer (she pats herself). Don't you ever get taken that way? When I can't see myself I begin to wonder if I really and truly exist. I pat myself to make sure, but it doesn't help much… When I talked to people I always made sure there was a mirror nearby in which I could see myself. I watched myself talking. And somehow it kept me alert, seeing myself as the others saw me…'

J.-P. SARTE, HUIS CLOS

~~~~~~~~~~~~

His form has passed away, he has become a mirror: naught is there but the image of another's face.

RUMI

~~~~~~~~~~~~

A sleepy-eyed grandmother
Encounters herself in an old mirror.
Clearly she sees a face,
But it doesn't resemble hers at all.

TOZAN RYOKAI

~~~~~~~~~~~~

After all, how long does a reflection remain in view? Make a practice of contemplating the origin of the reflection... This cheek and mole go back to the Source thereof.

RUMI

~~~~~~~~~~~

God's in, I'm out.

MEISTER ECKHART

~~~~~~~~~~~

Have you ever felt like nobody?
Just a tiny speck of air,
When everyone's around you,
And you are just not there.

KAREN CRAWFORD, AGED 9

SELF-IMAGE AND YOUR MANY-LEVELLED BODY-MIND

Other people see your face, your appearance, but you don't, except indirectly. You depend on reflections from others, from your environment, from mirrors and cameras to know who you are in the world. This is human self-consciousness: being aware of your appearance, of you-as-you-are-for-others.

As the above illustration shows, these images of yourself (changing as you grow older) occur to you as capacity, to you-as-you-are-for-yourself. You are faceless, yet at the same time you have in mind (you are capacity for) an image of your face - or of your body, your family, religion, nation, race... Your self-image at this level is human.

If you imagine the face of the planet you are still entertaining a self-image, but because this image is not human you may not think of it as yourself. Yet it is yourself: it is you from further away. At this range you are planetary. Entertaining any image of how you look, whether it's human, planetary, solar, cellular, atomic... is being self-conscious.

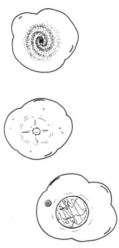

Who imagines these images? Who is self-conscious at all these different levels? You know yourself as a person, a planet, a star, a molecule... Who is the 'you', the reality behind your appearances? Point at the 'you' and see.

Body and Mind

Consider this way of distinguishing between 'mind' and 'body' (suggested by Douglas Harding):

My body is how I appear to others – the forms I take over there in their empty centres. I cannot see my body directly – I only know about it because others reflect it back to me. As others approach me I learn that they see this galaxy, this star, this planet, this species, this face, this cell... My body has layers. When others observe me from as near as possible, my body almost vanishes. When I observe myself at zero distance, my body completely vanishes. Here is the non-physical centre and source of all my physical appearances.

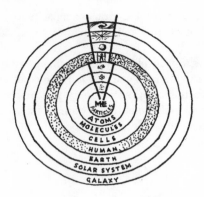

Illustration by Douglas Harding

My 'mind' is my view out – the content of this empty centre. Looking out at increasing distances from my empty centre into my world, I see my headless body, other people, other species, other planets, other stars… My mind has layers, like my body. My view out includes not only what I see, but also what I hear, taste, think, feel… At zero distance I find no content of any kind – no mind. Here I find the empty container and source of my world-wide mind.

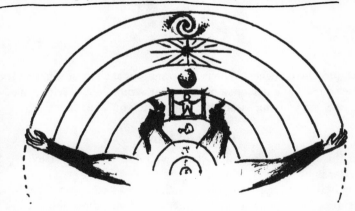

Illustration by Douglas Harding

The Mind Game

The mind game is a version of *the face game*. Playing *the mind game* is living and acting as if my mind is *here*, as if it is central, inside my head here, a thing that is separate from the world out there.

When I think about another person, or another planet, *where* are my thoughts? I find no mind or head at centre in which to keep them. My thoughts are centrifugal, connected to the objects I'm thinking about: my thoughts about another person connect to that person *there*; my thoughts about another planet connect to that planet *there*. In other words, my thoughts are at large, woven into the world: they are an aspect of the world, of my view out, rather than of a *central* self. (I find no central self.) However, in everyday conversation I divide the contents of my mind, my view out, into two kinds of things: things *physical* and things *mental*. I say that my desk, for example, is *physical* and is *outside* my head, but my thoughts about my desk are *mental* and are *inside* my head, separate from my desk by about half a metre. I do this because I know that others see my desk (and my head) but not my thoughts. Accepting the view that my mind is inside my head (and your mind is inside your head) is a useful convention when communicating with others. However, I am aware that my private reality is different. My thoughts about my desk *are not divided off* from my desk: they are not in my head but are in this boundless 'no-head', in this 'no-mind' in which I find both my thoughts and the world. I find no dividing line between inside and outside, between mind and world. What is your experience? Is your mind separate from your world?

It takes energy to play *the mind game* - to maintain the fiction that my thoughts are inside an imagined head here, separate from the rest of the world. And though it's a useful, indeed necessary convention for living in society, believing it is my private reality as well is not only tiring, but gets me into all kinds of trouble too. Under the illusion that my mind is all bottled up in a tiny container, it's no wonder if I feel depressed, lonely, isolated, alienated, uncreative, under pressure, angry, and sometimes quite mad. When I stop pretending and see my mind as it is, including *where* it is, I correct a fundamental mistake and heal a deep wound in my psyche – the wound of making a thing of my psyche and separating it from the world. This healing, this seeing through the illusion of being contained inside anything – this Liberation - releases energy, creativity and joy.

All this is for testing.

FOUR STAGES OF LIFE

Throughout our lives we're always two-sided. We always have both a public and a private identity. On the one hand we're individuals in the eyes of others, on the other hand we're capacity for the world. However, we're not always aware of our two-sided nature. There are potentially four main stages in our lives, and as we move through these stages our attention oscillates between our public and our private selves. Sometimes our focus is on one side, sometimes on the other. The four main stages of our lives are the baby, the child, the adult and the seer.

Stage One - The Baby

In the first stage of the baby we were unaware of our appearance, unaware of our public identity. We hadn't yet learned to see ourselves through the eyes of others. Conscious only of our own point of view, our private reality, we were faceless, at large, space for the world, without putting it in these or in any terms.

Stage Two - The Child

In the second stage of the child we were becoming aware of our public identity. Seeing ourselves more and more through the eyes of others, we began learning to take responsibility for ourselves as individuals. In the process we began overlooking our private reality. But our attention was inconsistent. Often we would forget about our public identity, completely losing ourselves in whatever we were doing. But as we grew older, these periods of unselfconscious openness and freedom came less often and went more quickly.

Stage Three - The Adult

In the third stage of the adult we identify profoundly with our public identity. Seeing ourselves as others see us, we're in no doubt at all that we are what we look like. In this stage we deny the reality of who we really are. It would seem that the price of genuinely becoming a person is the loss of our private self. We may not lose it for long, but lose it we must. Many benefits flow from becoming an individual, but though we may not know it, we're now cut off from our centre and source. It's not surprising if we find ourselves feeling that something isn't quite right, that we're missing something important.

Stage Four - The Seer

Fortunately this need not be the end of our journey. We can go on to the fourth stage of the seer where we discover the reality of our private Self and begin drawing on its immense healing power. Seeing who we really are at centre we now begin living a truly balanced two-sided life – private as well as public, public as well as private.

One of the good things about losing touch with our private Self as we grow up is that when we return to it we see it with fresh eyes. It seems that we have to leave Home before we can really appreciate how wonderful Home is. And because our individuality doesn't disappear when we see who we really are, we can now celebrate our one consciousness with many voices.

Seeing who we really are is a natural stage in our development. If we are not enjoying this fourth stage we are stopping short of our potential, like a rose bush growing, producing buds, but then not flowering.

The Awakening of Humanity

These stages are a map for each of us individually. They are also, in general terms, a map for ourselves as a species. In the distant past we were not very self-conscious: not having yet developed the art of seeing ourselves from outside, we didn't have a strong idea of being separate from the rest of the world.

More recently we have become highly conscious of our appearance, of being human and therefore separate from other species and the planet. (Identifying with the objective view of ourselves, we dismiss our original subjective view as 'primitive.') However, this narrow, exclusive, one-sided view of ourselves is now giving way to a combination of the objective and the subjective - a two-sided view. As well as being aware of what we look like at a certain range – our human identity – a growing number of us are also seeing who we really are, our central non-identity that, infinitely wide and deep, includes all beings, all things. This development suggests that as a species we are now moving into the next stage of consciousness. If you are seeing your true Self, you are evidence of this evolutionary change. Hopefully enough of us will see who we really are quickly enough to transform the way we as a species see ourselves - before our narrow, one-sided view causes us, and the rest of life, irreparable harm. Surely we can no longer go on with only a few of us enjoying Enlightenment. We need it to be the recognised norm. The survival of civilization and life as we know it may well depend on, if not the majority of us, at least an influential minority, awakening to and acting from our central, all-inclusive Self.

However, important as numbers are, it's not really a numbers game. When just one of us looks within and sees the one, indivisible Self that we all are, then she (or he) is seeing as and for all of us – though we may not know it, she knows it for us. We are all within the One that she is. In this sense, when any one of us awakens to our true Self, then that one – that One – gathers the rest of us up in his or her awakening – in the One's awakening to itself.

Seeing now the Light within yourself, you are seeing as and for us all. You are gathering us all up in the Light. Thank you!

The traditional demonstration of a baby's awareness of ME, the self-as-object, involves some red rouge. Experimenters hand a mother a cloth with the rouge on it and have her wipe her baby's nose, leaving a smudge that the baby is unaware of. The mother then places the child in front of a large mirror that rests on the floor. Before they are a year old, babies seem incapable of connecting the red nose in the mirror with themselves. If they're intrigued by it, they pat the mirror, as if the person there were another child. Starting at fifteen months, however, a few babies realize it's their nose that has the red spot and they reach not for the mirror but for their own face. By their second birthday, about three-quarters of the babies tested do so. Now they know who it is they're looking at in the mirror. They can also watch a videotape of themselves and say, 'That's Clare' or 'That's me'. They can do the same with pictures in a scrapbook. Though they're far from being able to reflect on themselves in a MENTAL mirror, they do have an I that can see ME.

JOHN KOTRE, WHITE GLOVES: HOW WE CREATE OURSELVES
THROUGH MEMORY (W.W. NORTON & CO.)

— EXPERIMENT 5 —

Two-Way Looking

Point at any object in front of you. At the same time point with your other hand back at yourself, at your no-face. Two-way pointing - and two-way looking: you are looking out at things and in at no-thing, out at colours and in at transparency, out at shapes and in at formlessness, out at movement and in at stillness.

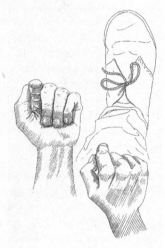

Do this in front of a mirror - face there to no-face here.

In a workshop, someone objected to the idea of two-way looking, saying that eyes can only look one way. Douglas Harding responded: 'But are you looking out of eyes? I am looking out of a single eye, and this eye is a wholly different kind of eye, and very special: it can look both out and in!'

Look for yourself and see if this is true.

PERFECT SEEING

However imperfect your view of things in the world, your view in to who you really are is always perfect. You see only a part of any thing at any one time – you see the front of your hand but not the back, or the cover of a closed book but not the open pages. But you see all of this seamless emptiness now. Nor can you see it differently from the way others see it, for there is nothing here to see differently. You don't see this Clarity more clearly than I see it, nor less clearly. Nor does it improve when you attend to it, nor deteriorate when you neglect it.

This is the one 'thing' you can never do wrong. Whatever you are doing, even if you're the best in the world, there will be times when you fall short of your ideal. But look within and your Seeing is perfect every time.

The outward and the inward man are as different as earth and heaven.

MEISTER ECKHART

~~~~~~~~~~~~~

Hsueh-feng went to the forest to cut trees with his disciple Chang-sheng. 'Don't stop till your axe cuts to the very centre of the tree,' warned the teacher.

THE IRON FLUTE

THE EXPERIENCE AND THE MEANING

The meaning of who we really are, without the experience, is a lot of words – words that confuse and divide as much as they clarify and unite. But the experience of who we really are without any meaning is 'So what?' We need both.

See, and you see the Self instantly and perfectly. Keep Seeing and find out what it means to you. However, unlike the experience, the meaning takes time to emerge and develop, and will never be complete – there will always be more to understand, more to feel. But because you see your Self perfectly, because you are all of the Self, now and forever, without having to do, think or feel anything in particular, without having to understand it, does it matter that your understanding is incomplete? Not in my view. And does it really matter that the insights that come to you, no matter how profound, always go? (If we don't let go of old insights, there's no room for new ones.) Practise two-way attention and observe that whilst meaning comes and goes, the source of meaning neither appears nor disappears. It's always here. And when an insight does fade and you experience a lack of meaning, a 'dry' period, carry on Seeing (for it's own sake, because it's the way things are, because it's the plain truth, even if for the time being it 'means nothing'), and find out whether or not new insights don't emerge from the Source, from this 'meaningless emptiness'. I find they always do. The Source is inexhaustible, forever bubbling up with fresh meaning.

The Meditation

(part one)

Douglas Harding, from *The Toolkit for Testing the Incredible Hypothesis*

Conscious 1st personhood (seeing Who you really are) is a kind of meditation (in an exact sense, the most radical sort). Its watch-word is SEE WHO'S HERE, and its distinctive marks (again, all are for you to try out) are that it is:

Down-to-earth. It works at least as well in the marketplace as in the meditation hall, when you are active as when you are resting, when your eyes are open as when they are shut.

Unwithdrawn. So far from requiring or inducing a somewhat trancelike state and temporary retirement from the world and from people, it sharpens your appreciation of what's going on. You are *more* alive and with it: Indeed you are the view, without being lost in it. It's not when you look at, but when you overlook, the Seer that the seen grows dim and distorted. Not only the 'outer' world, but also your 'inner' world of psychological states, is obscured when you ignore the Inmost which covers and underlies them all.

Voluntary. The initial seeing gives the ability to renew it. Since the Absence of things here is as plainly visible and as coolly factual as their presence there, the seeing of this Absence is available immediately, anytime, *at will*. Unlike ideas and feelings, you can have this simple seeing when you need it most, as when you are agitated or worried. It's ready to hand when dealing with troubles as they arise, on the spot.

Expressed physically. This meditation requires no special postures or physical skills. On the other hand, the physical effects can become very noticeable. Typically, they include an alert stillness, a muscular relaxation felt as energizing and not depleting, a marked slowing of the breath, a straightening and raising of the neck and spine. The complexion tends to clear, the eyes to shine, the general bodily tone to improve. Of course, you may find it easier to start at the physical end, and, when you are sitting, to sit up: this can indeed help you to see Who is sitting up.

Eventually continuous. There are no occasions when this meditation is inappropriate, no times when you may safely wander from the 1st-person position. In the end you stay at Home where it goes on unbroken, though at times unobtrusively, as the bass accompaniment in music.

Life-integrating. This way, your life isn't split into two compartments - a Self-aware (interior, meditative, religious) and a Self-unaware (exterior, discursive, secular) - worlds apart, not easily brought together and reconciled.

Foolproof. While it lasts, this is an all-or-nothing (actually, an All-and-Nothing) meditation which can't be done badly. You can't see half your Absence, nor can you half-see it. Either you are looking at What's central to you, or you are overlooking it.

Unmystical. This meditation is certainly not in itself a mystical or religious experience, not euphoric, not a sudden expansion into universal love or cosmic consciousness, not any kind of feeling or thought or intuition whatever. Quite the contrary, it is absolutely featureless, colourless, neutral. It is gazing into the pure, still, cool, transparent Fountainhead, and simultaneously out from It at the streaming, turbulent world - without being carried away into that world. You can ensure your full share of mystical or spiritual experiences, not by going downstream after them, but only by noticing that you are forever upstream of them all, and they can only be enjoyed there from their Source in you.

Unexplosive. It's true that the initial sight of your Source may come as a blazing, world-shaking revelation: and what event in your life, for sure, could better deserve such celebration? But these fireworks aren't necessary, and the display fizzles out soon enough anyhow. Many (if not most) serious practitioners of this meditation have come to it quietly, with some such remark as 'Why yes of course, that's exactly how it is here'. All depends on your individual temperament, upon your cultural-religious background and expectations, and above all upon how much tension, how much psychological stress has been built up - whether undeliberately in the course of ordinary life or deliberately by special religious disciplines and meditational practices.

Matter-of-fact. It is true, also, that the days or weeks or months following your initial seeing (whether it came explosively or not) are liable to prove joy-filled and light-some. You feel new-born into a new world. But sooner rather than later, alas, all this fades - much to your surprise and disappointment. 'It does *nothing* for me!' The temptation is then to give up the meditation, under the mistaken impression that you have lost the art of it. In fact, if you persist nevertheless, it comes to be valued less for its appetising but incidental fruits than for itself - for the plain and savourless truth of it, for the nothing which it does indeed do for you, instead of the something it used to do - and this is a great advance. Beginning to lose interest in the fruits, you ensure they grow all the more healthily, unobserved and undisturbed, and ripen in season. Meantime, and always, your sole business is their nourishing Root.

Unifying. Only in this Root, only as this Root, are we all One and the Same forever. This meditation infallibly unites you with all creatures at the one Spot where all converge, where we are at last wholly relieved of those manifest peculiarities and hidden feelings and thoughts which distinguish and part us from one another. The Void, just because It really is void, is identical in all beings everywhere and at all times. If It could be experienced as loving in me, bright in you, and specially empty in him, It would only serve to thrust us still further apart. But in fact you are him and me, without the slightest doubt or anxiety, directly you find the Spot where there's Nothing to come between us.

HOMEWORK

- Spend a few minutes looking in a mirror, consciously leaving your face out there where it belongs. See that you are empty for that face - there is absolutely nothing your side of the mirror. As you do this, be aware of your responses, your thoughts and feelings. There is no 'right' response, just your unique and special one.
- Continue pointing at your facelessness several times a day to remind yourself to See.
- Sit for ten minutes, eyes open, consciously looking out of your edgeless single Eye. Keep bringing your attention back to this clear Window whenever you find yourself overlooking it.
- When insights and feelings fade, stay conscious of who you really are.

CHAPTER THREE

SEEING FOR THE BLIND

In this and following chapters I include comments from people who participated in the course I offered on the internet. These comments show how quickly and easily people get the point of Seeing.

Sometimes people object that Seeing is too visual. What if someone is blind? How do you share Seeing with them?

A good person to ask is someone who is blind.

In-Seeing Experiments For The Blind

Allan Jones

Like many other people, I have been knocked clean off my perch by Douglas Harding's teachings – especially as presented in his experiments. When I first tried the most basic of these experiments, the in-pointing finger, it was with little hope of anything significant happening. This was because I had been blind for several years. But to my astonishment, I 'saw' what was intended: empty capacity.

When I tried to make sense of this experience, I thought at first that this 'seeing' must be contingent on my once having been sighted. I had in fact used visual memory to conjure up the image of an in-pointing finger. I found myself wondering if the same experiment would work for a person born blind. I also began to think about possible supplementary experiments for blind people.

I soon concluded that a person born blind would indeed be able to experience the deep meaning of the in-pointing finger. In fact, it might be suggested that such a person could have an odd sort of advantage in the in-pointing experiment, as compared with sighted folk. To understand this, it is necessary to grasp what 'pointing' means to the congenitally blind.

If you as a sighted person point at an object, you identity or single out that object within a visual array. And you establish direct sensory contact with it through vision. When a blind man points toward that same object, in response to an instruction such as 'thirty degrees left', he does not sensorally find it or contact it. He only indicates its general direction. To the blind man himself, the object does not yet exist. The directional indication 'exists', for him, as an experience of kinesthesis - as the introsensed orientation of his arm/hand/finger.

But what this pointing really amounts to, at a level of consciousness deeper than introsensing or the five external senses, is a vectoring of the arrow of attention. Consciousness is directed outward, in a state of expectation, anticipating a potential object. When Douglas invites the blind man to turn that finger around and attend to what is doing the attending, something happens that has nothing to do with objects.

Twisting his hand and finger about so that consciousness now says 'attention inward', the man finds - as always - that the finger poised in space does not pin down an object. The pointing finger finds no-thing, no-I, in this zone of feeling where an embodied I is supposed to reside.

This is a revelation. The blind man's limitation, his non-seeing of things, has been transmuted into the seeing of no-thing.

If the basic principle of noumenal seeing is the reversal of the arrow of attention, it should be possible to devise more experiments that re-orient that arrow in non-visual ways. When I thought about this, it seemed important that experimental design take account of the special significance of the head.

A finger pointing at one's own head can pack a noumenal whallop because of our common assumption that the head is the locus of the I. We implicitly define the I as the perceiver or knower, and it is the head that contains all the organs of perceiving/knowing except for generalised touch.

This is true as well for blind people, who lack only the visual mode of knowing. As perceiver in the mode of listening, tasting and smelling, and above all as the thinker who processes touch information, the blind person implicitly locates 'I' exactly where a sighted person does - just behind his forehead.

The point of many of Douglas's experiments is to reveal the non-existence of this capitated or heady I. So I decided that my experiments too would direct attention first outward from the head, then back toward it.

The following two experiments can be done by blind or sighted people, the latter with eyes closed. A blind person would access these experiments on cassette tape, just as I did with a transcription of *Head Off Stress*. As a sighted reader you can transcribe these experiments onto tape or have a friend read them to you. If a friend isn't available, reading through what follows will at least give you the general idea of how these non-visual experiments work.

The first one relies upon introsensing; the second utilises hearing.

— EXPERIMENT 1—

Real Seeing

Raise one hand and make a fist, as though preparing for one-handed boxing. Position the fist out in front of the face as though to protect it from a blow. Throughout this experiment you can most easily hold your fist up if your elbow is supported. For example, fold one arm over your stomach and use the back of that hand to support the elbow of the arm that's making a fist. Make the fist tightly enough that it produces a feeling of concentrated pressure, but not so tightly that it is painful or difficult to maintain.

Hold that fist up there and direct your full attention upon it, taking in that sensation of bunched-up pressure as intently as you can. Continue this for a moment or two, until that sense of pressure out there is sharp, clear, and all-absorbing.

Now suddenly reverse the arrow of your attention so that it points not outward to the fist, but inward. That's right - just turn your perception around 180 degrees and realise what's doing the perceiving. See what's right here inside.

Yes. What's here is awareness, pure and simple. What's on show is consciousness itself, blaringly obvious and immediate. See it as the unobstructed clearness that accommodates those fist-feelings. See it as the pool of awareness in which those fist sensations float. See that this pool has a definite, almost tingling presence. It is Presence itself, intense living water.

Now see what has happened to the distinction between inside and outside. It is not that the fist is out there, and the perceiving consciousness in here. There is only one place, this clear pool of awareness, and it contains that fist.

Unclench the fist, slowly, and attend to where this action is taking place - within awareness. Now extend that arm, seeing the sensations unfold within that same awareness.

This is real seeing. It is not seeing with the eyes, which usually look out in search of all the things we are not. It is instead the direct seeing of what we really are. We are aware capacity, this intensely present know-thing that accommodates all things whatsoever. We are the empty consciousness in which things appear, replaced by other things in regular succession.

That hand you call your own, and all the other body parts you call yours, are among those things that come and go. What's taking them all in, this unobstructed consciousness, is the real you. It does not come and go: it always is.

— EXPERIMENT 2—

Real Hearing

Once again, raise one hand in front of your face, its palm facing inward toward you. This time, instead of making a fist, extend the fingers downwards so that your fingertips rest comfortably on your palm.

Hold your hand there, concentrating upon it. Feel the warmth of your palm under those snuggly-tucked fingers. Feel the tiny touch sensations where your fingers nudge and slightly overlap each other, and where your thumb rests lightly against your forefinger. Be aware of any vagrant throbbings or ticklings in that hand. Be aware of the whole hand as a little nest of warmth, pressure and touch.

Now, once again, turn the arrow of your attention right around so that it points inward. Be aware of the clear consciousness that's taking in that hand. See how its emptiness is completely open and available for the snug fullness of the hand. And see once again that the hand floats in awareness, like a warmly-buzzing fish in cool limpid water.

Now use that hand to make a sound. Scoop your fingertips briskly across your palm from the base of the palm upwards. This makes a small rubbing or whishing sound. Repeat this sound as a regular beat or pulse, listening all the while.

Listen to where this sound is. See that the sound is taking place within awareness, just as those warm buzzing sensations floated in this same awareness. Continue to make the sound, and see that the sound is bordered on every side by a receptive silence. This is the empty but aware silence that allows that sound to be heard.

Now stop the sound. Hear the silence right where the sound was. Listen to that silence, for a long moment. See that the silence is not just in this awareness, it is this awareness. Awareness and silence are one. Listen to it.

Now hear how any small, distant sound - birdsong, a voice in another room, a car engine in the street - arises out of that silence and falls back into it. And hear how any small continuing sound, such as the rumble of your furnace or the hum of your refrigerator, is heard against the silence. It is this silent awareness that allows that sound to be.

How could it be otherwise? You, as consciousness itself, must be no-thing in order that things consciously register. So too you must be essentially silence at the core, in order that sounds appear.

Hearing this silence is real hearing. It is the hearing of what we really are, a quiet stillness that is peace itself.

It is the Unborn which sees and hears, eats and sleeps

BANKEI

~~~~~~~~~~~~~~

I look and listen without using eyes and ears.

LIEH-TZU

~~~~~~~~~~~~~~

By what means does this body or mind perceive? Can they perceive with the eyes, ears...? No. Your own Nature, being essentially pure and utterly still, is capable of this perception.

HUI-HAI

~~~~~~~~~~~~~~

You each have a pair of ears, but what have you ever heard with them? You each have a tongue, but what have you ever said with it?... From whence, then, do all these forms, voices, odours, and tastes come?

FO-YEN

~~~~~~~~~~~~~~

Only God has seeing, hearing.

AL-ARABI

Thought-Bees

If thoughts were bees,
who would dare to shut them
tight in the hive of the head?
He who shatters
this hive of pretence
with the swift hammer of seeing
sees no box, no house,
no door to lock.
The spell of images is broken
and the swarm
breaks out
to scatter in the world.
The hive of nothingness
brings to the world
the honey of love,
and thought-bees,
watched by the queen
of the eye, roam free.

COLIN OLIVER

~~~~~~~~~~~~~~

See, where thou nothing seest;
Go, where thou canst not go;
Hear, where there is no sound;
Then where God speaks art thou.

ANGELUS SILESIUS

~~~~~~~~~~~~~~

As rivers lose name and shape in the sea, wise men lose name and shape in
God, glittering beyond all distance.

MUNDAKA UPANISHAD

~~~~~~~~~~~~~~

If the soul would but stay within, she would have everything.

MEISTER ECKHART

COURSE COMMENTS

I first turned my finger around and thought, 'Well, of course I can't see my face';

and then I went into my old meditation trick of kinda stepping out of my line of vision and being able to 'see' with my inner eye what I looked like. But I realised that this wasn't the point either to the exercise. I was a little baffled at first by just 'what' I was supposed to be 'seeing'. Then reading your exercise over and over I came to understand somewhat and I did the exercise again.

This time I was staring out of a huge window (as you described), only it appeared to me like a bay window but without any panes, just like a rounded window which fades into nothingness and joins with the world. I could see some of my hair which framed the 'window' like curtains, and my nose slightly, and if I looked up I could see a shadow of my eyebrows and forehead, like the tops of the 'curtains'. But here I was/am looking out from nothingness, and I feel very free. I can take it all into my no-thing and experience it all.

Donna

———

I liked the closed-eyes experiments in today's lesson - really helped me be with sensation and the way in which awareness embraces all sensation.

———

Hello, I have also just worked on the first lesson and as always I am struck by the effectiveness of its ability to remind me where and what I am. There is something remarkable and deeply relieving about being emptiness and witnessing everything unfolding out of the empty space where my head used to be. I'm looking forward to the other lessons and to sharing the experience with others.

Ian

The Meditation

(part two)

Douglas Harding, from *The Toolkit for Testing the Incredible Hypothesis*

Democratic. One welcome consequence is that among those who faithfully practise this meditation there can be no hierarchy or pecking-order, no gurus or chelas, no spiritual one-upmanship and intimidation. Indeed, what other sure basis of human equality (not to say democracy) could there be but this - our common Identity?

Egoless. Nothing is achieved, but only discovered. And What's discovered is totally humbling: your Nothingness when actually seen (and not merely entertained or believed in) can't be doubted. This alone carries conviction. Here is the one Spot, the Spot where you are real and no appearance, which is plainly free from egotism and everything else - in a word, *free*.

Safe. This meditation is safe, not only because it can't be bungled, not only because it avoids dependence upon others on the one hand and self-pride on the other, but also because it is uncontrived. There's nothing arbitrary or fanciful about it, nothing to strain your credulity, nothing to go wrong, nothing to set you apart from ordinary people, nothing special. It is safe because it is finding out how matters stand, not trying to manipulate them. What could be less dangerous than ceasing to deceive yourself about your Self, or more dangerous than not doing so?

Natural. Though notably natural from the start, this meditation gets more so, and in the end entirely so. At first you probably need little reminders to bring you to your senses - such as counting your eyes (what eyes?) and getting face-to-no-face with a friend. But in time (not necessarily reckoned in years) these devices are dispensed with: 1st-personhood becomes second nature (or first Nature regained) and the last thing you do is go around preoccupied with your facelessness. It's much simpler than that - more like resting at Home in Home's superbly clear air, without any thoughts about it at all. Just as no man loiters in the hall studying the front door he's just come in by, but goes on to enjoy the comforts indoors, so you come to enjoy the Immensity within, and these little gates to It are recognised to be the paltry and temporary contrivances - indeed gimmicks - which they are. (Many traditional religious devices are so complicated or mysterious or beautiful or impressive that they divert attention from their underlying purpose, and the means have come to replace the end. Hopefully the blatant triviality of our gadgets will render them less likely, in the course of centuries, to evolve into sacred objects credited with value in themselves.)

Not exclusive. This meditation doesn't preclude, and need not interfere with, any other kind of meditation - such as 'sitting meditation' or za-zen - which you may find helpful. What is does rule out is meditation which assumes the meditator isn't already at Home.

Autonomous. Because this meditation is quite ordinary - secular, simple, obvious, commonplace - and because there's precisely Nothing to be learned, no expert guidance is needed, no meditation manuals or masters, no agonising choice between their often conflicting systems, no hunting for the infallible Teacher - seeing He's located right where you already are. On the other hand, the company of friends who are engaged in this meditation is both helpful and delightful.

Infectious. And in the beginning a friend is practically indispensable. It is very rare for the initial seeing to occur spontaneously: nearly everyone is initiated into this mediation by someone who is already doing it, for the condition is highly infectious, a direct person-to-person transmission. Books have proved almost - if not quite - incapable of this transmission: their job is to awaken the desire to discover Who is reading the book, and to confirm the discovery once it has been made.

Unself-conscious. The principle of this mediation is: never lose sight of your Self in any circumstances, and your problems are taken care of - including, strange to say, the problem of self-consciousness. *For finding the Self is losing the self.* Our meditation cures bashfulness, not by enabling you to lose yourself in the objective world, but by enabling you to find yourself - as its Container.

Paradoxical. Inconsistent and hard to please, you demand a meditation which detaches you from all creatures yet unites you with them, which reduces you absolutely yet exalts you absolutely, which makes you wholly present and self-aware yet wholly absent and self-forgetful, which gives you rest yet inspires action, which is aimless yet purposeful, which leaves you nothing to do because you are already at the goal yet everything to do because you are still at the beginning. What's wanted, in short, is a meditation which reconciles all your built-in contradictions. An impossibly tall order! Nevertheless - wonder of wonders - this is just the meditation which our hypothesis ['Closer is He than breathing, nearer than hands and feet'], put into everyday practice, has to offer!

Fascinating. And you can go on tirelessly with this meditation because it is so interesting, and it is so interesting because it is the ever-renewed discovery of What, after all, concerns you most. If this Subject isn't your business, what is? It wouldn't be surprising if every other subject of meditation were in the end to fail to hold your attention. But how could this Inside Story, this very Core of you, always the same yet always fascinatingly new, ever be rivalled or ever fail you? How could you ever get to the end of Its indescribable, breath-taking mystery?

Two-directional. Above all, this meditation, Janus-like, faces both ways. Simultaneously looking in at the Seer and out at the seen, it takes in and makes sense of the seen because it puts No-thing in its way - and gives priority to this No-thing. Seek the 1st person and the 3rd shall be added. Seek the 3rd, and even that shall be taken away.

— EXPERIMENT 6 —

The Card

The Card experiment draws attention to the contrast between your appearance and your reality.

Cut out a face-sized hole in a piece of a card roughly 45 x 30 cm. Attach a small mirror to the bottom right-hand corner.

Look in the mirror and notice where your face is: out there in the mirror, not here above your shoulders. As in Experiment 4, bring the mirror towards and away from you and see how your appearance changes. Although your mirror reveals what you are at different distances, obviously it does not reveal what you are at centre.

Notice that your face is a thing and is therefore separate from other things. It is only itself and has room for nothing but itself.

Now look at the hole in the card. There's no face there, just space – it's empty and clear. Because the hole is empty it is also full – it is capacity for the scene beyond. Being nothing, it is unconditionally open and receptive for whatever is presented in it.

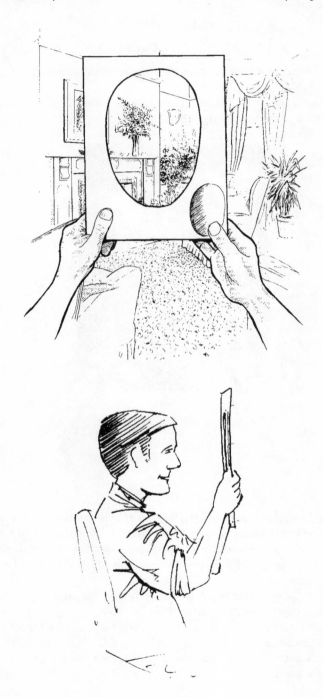

Bring the card towards you – the size of the hole grows, so containing more of the room.

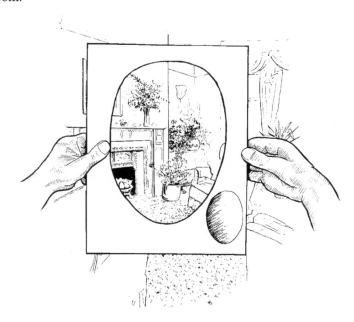

Bringing the card closer you see the hole continuing to grow, including more and more of the room. Then the card begins to disappear.

Bring the card right up to you and put it on.

The card has vanished. All that remains is the now edgeless hole which is full of the room. You are seeing what you are at no distance – capacity for the world. Your no-face takes in and receives the world unconditionally.

Of course you are aware that for others you are not capacity for the world – you are a person with a card round your face! You have two sides to yourself: publicly you are in the world, privately the world is in you.

REFLECTION

We are good at attending to things in the world, especially at about arm's length. It's the region where we socialise, use phones, keyboards and cutlery, drive and so on. We need to be attentive at this distance to survive - and, of course, at other distances too. But we are not so attentive to ourselves at zero distance. Perhaps we think there's no practical or survival value in looking here. Anyway, convinced we already know what we are at centre, we don't bother to look.

In this experiment we bother to look. We start by looking in the region where we are good at looking: at arm's length. Then, as we bring the card towards us, we keep looking. We don't stop looking when the card is a few centimetres away, convinced we know what we are going to find, nor do we turn to someone else and ask them their opinion of what we are at centre. No, we follow the card all the way home to the place we are looking out of, and we look for ourselves into this special place – a place that is unlike any other place in the whole world.

The card is a vehicle that transports us from there to here, from our periphery to our centre, from the domain of appearances to the domain of Reality.

In his book *The Little Book of Life and Death* Douglas Harding calls this experiment *Putting On Immortality*. Once more hold the card out in front of you. Your face in the mirror is mortal, as is the card and all the things you can see in the hole. But the hole is not a mortal thing – the hole will not age or die. Now put the card on. Your face in the mirror vanishes along with the card. In other words, you don't put your *mortal face* on here, you put your *immortal no-face* on.

Each time you look here, you visit (move back into) the home you never really left, your *eternal* home, and enjoy a unique view from this unique residence!

When this perishable one puts on imperishability, and this mortal one puts on immortality, then Death is swallowed up in victory. O Death, where is your sting? O Grave, where is your victory?

ST PAUL

COURSE COMMENTS

This is a wonderful class, thank you for teaching it. I have always felt an emptiness inside myself. I have tried to fill it to no avail. Now I realize that this emptiness is not something to be filled. It is where my consciousness should be. I feel whole now, not so much of an outsider as I always have. I am part of the universe just as much as the universe is part of me! Thank you so much for helping me out of the box I was trapped in.

Violet

Your exercise for the eyes was quite a surprise for me. Like most people, I had always considered my view to be the result of two eyes seeing rather than a 'single eye' or 'whole' view. Interesting … VERY interesting!

Van

———

Thank you for helping me see that there is no other experience to search for to prove that I have reached 'enlightenment'. Your teaching today showed me clearly that I need not be defined by my experiences, but contain all experience. When I identify with the source of all experience, that is enlightenment.

Kim

HOMEWORK

- Meditate with your eyes closed for ten minutes, aware of being the space in which everything is coming and going.
- Open your eyes and meditate for another five minutes - awake to being edgeless capacity for the scene, for feelings, for sounds.
- Share the card experiment with a friend.
- Continue pointing back at your no-face from time to time, attending to where your finger is pointing.

CHAPTER FOUR

REVIEW

So far you have considered the onion-like system of appearances that others see when they observe you – your many-levelled body. Then you pointed in to the source of all your appearances, your transparent centre. Looking out from your centre, you see that your world is arranged in layers, from your headless body to the stars – your many-levelled mind.

You have seen that the mirror confirms not only *what* your appearances are, but also *where* they are.

As well as seeing, you have investigated what you are with your eyes closed.

You have reflected on the four stages of your life: you began as a headless baby and evolved through childhood to become an adult fully identified with your appearance, with your public identity. Now, aware of who you really are, you are conscious both of your original Self and your acquired self – you are both divine and human.

You have also read what mystics say about the Self they see within themselves – the same Self that you see within yourself. And, reading the comments from the internet course, you know that many people today are seeing who they really are.

In this chapter we will explore how Seeing opens up a new way of being with others – the *face to no-face* way. The experiment that leads us into this is the Tube experiment. Following this are more comments from fellow seers plus another article by Douglas Harding on the benefits that flow from this two-way meditation.

— EXPERIMENT 7—

The Tube

This important experiment is worth taking the trouble to set up and do. It's a two-person experiment, so you will need to find a friend to do it with. And you will need a paper tube. Either cut the end off a paper bag or get a large piece of paper and tape the sides together to make a tube – about 45cm long and wide enough to fit your face into one end and your friend's face into the other end. Either have a third person read out the questions whilst you do the experiment with your friend, or if you don't have someone to help you, read a question out loud to yourself and your friend, go in the tube together and investigate, come out and read the next question, go back in the tube, and so on. Take your time, there's no hurry.

This is not a communication exercise, so you don't have to talk in the tube or even smile – simply look to see what is true. You don't even have to look in the other person's eyes if you don't want to.

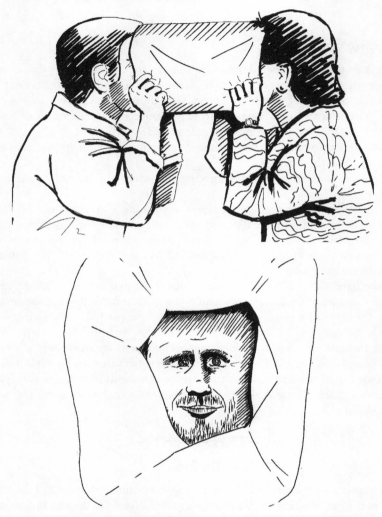

Let's begin. Put your face in one end of the tube whilst your friend puts her face in the other end. Be comfortable and answer (not out loud) the following questions:

- On present evidence, how many faces do you see in the tube, two or one?
- You can see your friend's face at the far end – do you see your face at the near end?
- Isn't your end wide-open? Doesn't the tube vanish into *nothingness* at your end – into clear, boundless consciousness?

- How many clear, boundless consciousnesses do you see in the tube, two or one?
- Is this single, undivided consciousness at the near end separate from the face at the far end? Is there a dividing line between this space and that face?
- As this space, aren't you built open for your friend, face there to no face here?
- Having no face of your own, couldn't you say that your friend's face is yours?
- Haven't you always been face to no-face with others?

Come out of the tube.
Spend a few moments exchanging your reflections about the experience.

REFLECTION

Although this experience is non-verbal, it's natural to want to describe it in words – words that will be different for each of us. But although we use different words, surely everyone has the same *experience* in the tube – face there to no face here.

As well as being non-verbal, this experience is also non-emotional. When we look at another person, of course we have feelings, but however we react, do we ever confront another person face to face? I don't. Seeing I am face there to no face here is not dependent on how I feel. Even when I am afraid, I'm still face to no-face.

How does being consciously *face to no-face* affect the way we relate to others?

Let's say I am not aware of who I really am. Pretending I have a face here, I play *the face game* (without realising I'm playing a game). My relationships are profoundly affected by this. For example, when I meet you I treat you the way I treat myself, as if you are behind your face there. Though I don't put it into words, my behaviour communicates my belief that we confront each other face to face, that you are contained inside your head and body there, just as I am here. You receive this message loud and clear. If you are also unaware of your true Self, then not only do you take on board my message, you send the same message to me so that together we re-enforce this mutual pretence of confrontation. It's a wonder if this doesn't lead to conflict.

But when I see that I have no face, not only do I see who *I* really am, I see who *you* really are too, for seeing *my* true Self is seeing *your* true Self – the space here is one, the One Self in all. Now my non-verbal message to you is: 'Like me, you are faceless. We are not confronting each other but are taking each other in.' In other words, 'I am you and you are me.' You are likely to sense 'where I am coming from'. If you are also aware of 'where *you* are coming from', then you cannot help but transmit the same non-verbal message to me. Together we now see and enjoy the reality of non-confrontation, the reality of trading faces, the reality of being each other. It's a wonder if this doesn't lead to love!

However, our own Seeing is not dependent on sharing it with others, welcome and supportive as this sharing is. Whether another person agrees or disagrees with you about being the One makes no difference to your own seeing that you are the One. The existence and nature of the One is self-evident and not dependent on outside confirmation. Indeed there can be no outside confirmation since there is no outside and there are no others. When you see you are the One, you see you are everywhere and alone.

COURSE COMMENT

The thought occurred to me that face to no-face could be an incredible tool to use in mediation work. As a state court judge who has to deal with conflict on a daily basis, I have found that so many of the experiments help me in dealing with it all without becoming jaded. Especially, though, it seems that face to no-face is an excellent way of helping disputing people to resolve amicably their differences.

I refer many cases to mediation, with mixed results. But it seems that if mediation could be done with a skilled mediator who could get the disputing parties to lose their faces, real progress could be made in the effort to find peace, even if it is at the local level. But perhaps that is where it has to start anyway. I'm curious if you know of anyone who has attempted this in mediation work, and especially how it could be approached. The area where it might be most applicable is in domestic relations. But it also could be very helpful in any number of other types of disputes as well, both legal and non-legal.

William

Marriage

(For Carole)

To see your face
with the eye of emptiness
is to have your face
as my own, and to find
between seeing and loving
not even a hairbreadth.

COLIN OLIVER

~~~~~~~~~~~~

As long as I am this or that, I am not all things.

MEISTER ECKHART

~~~~~~~~~~~~

Turn your face towards your own Face – you have no kinsman but yourself.

RUMI

~~~~~~~~~~~

Love your neighbour as yourself.

JESUS

~~~~~~~~~~~

Fear comes when there is a second.

BRIHADARANYAKA UPANISHAD

~~~~~~~~~~~

The one principle of hell is – 'I am my own!'

GEORGE MACDONALD

COURSE COMMENTS

I have been having a very intense experience as a result of this course. Everything has changed, everything is the same. I have been practising being headless with other people and find a more positive response. I have more energy, more joy. It really is very delightful. I love it. I was ready for it.

———

My ability to relax into space deepens and the immediacy and newness of the space is as sharp and fresh now as the first time I was consciously aware of it.

———

You've just reminded me of a saying by Nisargadatta Maharaj: 'Wisdom tells me I am Nothing, Love tells me I am everything. Between the two my life flows.'

———

I feel more connected to everything around me. The perception that everything is within me is new to me.

Space embraces everything. I'm a therapist and often find myself sitting with people in pain and distress. In allowing the sense of space to fill the room all is somehow held and okay.

———

I have found in just the few days that I have been being in this space that is me that the past does drop away. Being in the present is so natural.

———

Last night I was by the seaside, watching the waves rolling in by moonlight, and there was the sense of its rolling into me, or within me – hard to describe.

———

I experienced headlessness years ago at a Jean Klein seminar but never really knew what it was and it passed after a few weeks. The experiments have given me a better handle.

———

I find that headlessness is very special when I'm walking along the beach. I feel as if I'm very tall, huge, really large enough to contain everything. And I really am 'riding the wind' as Lieh Tzu did. I'm just consciousness with the ocean and the sand moving in me.

———

Tomorrow I am definitely going to the beach. I can't wait to experience being headless at the beach!

———

What often feels extraordinary to me – though it's completely natural – is how flexible or adaptable I am when I am aware of this – especially when certain stuck states arise. They're easier to let go of. There's much greater ease.

———

Thank you so much for these remarkably articulate, effective, and easy to follow lessons. The first lesson came early, when I realized what my expectations of the class reflected about my idea of myself. I thought 'seeing who you really are' would be a class on recognizing which qualities of our personality are genuinely there and which are only make believe, i.e. this class was going to help me see what the real qualities of my personality were like. Instead, I found out that it was not focused directly on the contents of my mind or the qualities of my personality, but on the experiencer of the personality and the contents of the mind. How wonderful, and effortless. Another affirmation that awareness, direct experience, is what it's all about. Speculation leads to speculation, awareness leads to awareness. I truly am grateful to you for putting this class together, and wish that many others (or the rest of myself) find this wonderful discovery.

Asaf

———

Thank you very much for the wonderful experience. I see now that I see this place of Nothingness but I have a habit of dismissing it. I automatically move my attention from there. Seeing this place, I experience being, knowing. I always wondered what being, knowing is. Now I have a new notion of it. In Hebrew the word 'seeing' contains (is derived from) the word 'wisdom'. Thank you.

Rachel

———

I remember that book very well – *The Mind's I*. That's how I found out about headlessness. I saw the book with its beckoning eye on the cover, opened the chapter entitled *On Having No Head* and was struck forever, right in the bookstore. I looked up, and couldn't see my head and said/thought 'Wow!, is this it?'

Immediately I went to the comments and thought they didn't have much to do with the content in Harding's text. I don't remember either what it said exactly, but I remember thinking something like, 'These people are not talking about the same thing I just read about.'

Although I have always felt that the comments did a disservice to the selection of '*On Having No Head*', at the same time I am very grateful to *The Mind's I* for having existed.

Elsa

———

Today I am enamored with the newness of Seeing. How everything is new in it, how it never gets old. Then when I forget, I completely forget. When it visits again, innocently scooping me away, it is like the first time ever, and I can't believe that I could forget, that I could fail to keep my door open to this awareness all the time. But of course, fail I do.

Then, the business of growth. How Seeing grows. How, for me, it slowly percolates through the different strata of my self. (Are they really strata?) And I don't know where it will take me, or when, if at all.

Elsa

Individual Results

Douglas Harding, from The Toolkit for Testing the Incredible Hypothesis

What is this two-way, mundane meditation likely to do for one, how much difference does it make? In other words, what is it like to begin to live with our hypothesis, to make it actual and no longer hypothetical? No doubt each practitioner's story is unique, and one must expect many surprises. The following account, because it is based on the experience of a limited (but fast-growing) group of friends over a mere decade or so, [this was written in the early 1970s] is provisional and incomplete, and needs checking and supplementing by everyone who finds this message worth pursuing and practising.

In so far as one sees clearly and steadily into one's Void Nature, into how it is right here and now, what happens is this:

One's senses waken. Colours, textures, sounds, tastes, smells – all sensations are apt to take on a new brilliance, poignancy, novelty, in the sharpest contrast to their plain Background here. For instance, it is common (even when one has just begun to see) to find colours – such as the traffic lights and neon signs of cities at night, and their reflections in wet pavements and the sides of taxis – unbelievably glowing and beautiful.

One's heart goes out to the world. The more I take care of the Coolness here the more the warmth takes of itself there. It's not that I feel myself to be more loving (my love goes out to you and cannot be retained here) but that you are seen to be more lovable. My feelings, adhering now to their objects instead of their Subject (Who finds nothing here to attach them to) become real and spontaneous feelings and no longer put-on or worked-up, sentimental ones. [This] discovery … extends into the whole of life. Ceasing to cultivate and wallow in my own states – an anxious, self-defeating, absurd habit – I'm free at last to enjoy people and the world just as they come, from this their Empty Source. In other words, my mind, with all its thoughts and feelings, is centrifugal. Ceasing to be a small, local, private, personal possession abstracted from the universe there and shut up in a brain-box here (as if it could be!) my mind is at large, one with the universe, blown sky-high. The world, so seen, is the same old world, yet utterly different. It is replete with a mind and meaning I no longer abstract from it. It is all there, because I claim none of it for myself. It is sane. It makes sense. It is loved.

One's mind awakens. Ideas, inspiration, guidance from moment to moment, flow without obstruction from their Source, which is experienced here as Itself mindless. Paradoxically, to be really creative, to be really intelligent about things there, one must be a conscious numb-skull here, empty-headed, clueless, blank.

One's day-to-day problems are sorted out. These range from finding a parking place to deciding where to live, from how to get rid of mice to how to get on with one's mother-in-law. *Their answer is to see Who has them.* Then they – the problems - are removed rather than abolished, placed rather than solved; but this placing is, in effect, their solution. Here, one is shot of all problems. Minding one's own Business here, one notes with interest events there, and what one is led to do about them. The result may be surprising, mysterious, even shocking or absurd, but in the long run it shows a wisdom, an uncanny prescience, far beyond mere human computation. When at last, baffled and exhausted, one has the good sense to hand over from one's human computer (which takes account of only a fraction of the relevant data), to one's Universal Computer, to the Void Itself (which takes account of all the data), the answers that come out are the right ones. Not man, but the One who lives in man, knows best. So he finds when he abandons his imagined self to his true Self. The radical answer to every problem is never to lose sight of this Self in any circumstances.

Whatever the problem there, its solution lies here, at 180 degrees to it: the one-way, direct approach is never good enough. Perseus's problem was Medusa – to view her directly was to be made into stone, so he turned round and viewed her indirectly, mirrored in the shield given to him by the Goddess of Wisdom, and was safe. Similarly the world and its faces cease to petrify me – making me into a mere 3rd person, a face among faces and a thing among things – once I turn to What mirrors the world here so clearly. Only the 1st person, the No-thing, can cope with 2nd and 3rd persons, with things.

One's unconscious is taken care of. Only the No-mind can cope with the mind – conscious and unconscious. Another ancient myth puts the whole matter beautifully. An Eastern King sent his son down to Egypt to find the Pearl of Self-knowledge. Arrived there, he ate the food and wore the clothes of the Egyptians till he became drugged and forgot Who he was and why he was in Egypt. His Father, hearing of this, sent a bird-messenger to remind him, and the Prince set out to find the Pearl. Eventually he learned that it lay at the bottom of a lake, guarded by a terrible serpent. Braving the monster, he dived in, snatched the Pearl, and returned with it to his Father's house, on the way there donning his blue robe – the starry firmament.

Note that the Prince neither ignores nor takes on the serpent (his own unconscious, demonic, animal nature) but by-passes it. If one *fights* the serpent (as in direct moral discipline), he's always about to give in but never actually does so; and if one makes friends and *parleys with* the serpent (as in the many varieties of psychological exploration and analysis), he's delighted to keep up the dialogue indefinitely – and meantime to sit snugly on the Pearl. But if, like our hero, one creeps by the serpent when he's least alert and seizes the Pearl, one is then armed with the perfect dragon-taming charm. The sword of discipline only scratched and stimulated him, friendly overtures only encouraged him to keep one talking for life, but the talisman of Self-knowledge he respects. It doesn't allow one to ignore him (quite the contrary) nor is he reduced overnight to a pussy-cat (indeed he can put up a show of angry violence at the loss of his Jewel) but he knows his Master – and how to serve Him.

Take any psychological trouble large or small – for example, one's irritability, one's meanness, one's fear of spiders and of heights, one's anxiety that one isn't loving enough. The cure of the trouble isn't to go *into it* out of Oneself, nor to *retreat from it* into Oneself, but to *face it* from Oneself – to *look into it* from Here, consciously to view it from this trouble-free Home whose windows open wide and clear onto the troubled scene. As always, the solution is two-way looking, seeing simultaneously what one's looking at and What one's looking out of – face to No-face, thing to No-thing, *problem to No-problem.* This therapy works because it fits the facts, for in truth one can never leave Home, nor shut out the view from Home, nor separate them.

One ceases playing games. The basic move in all the tragi-comic games one plays is pretending to leave Home, stationing oneself in imagination over there and turning in upon oneself and putting on a face here – putting on some particular act and its masks for the benefit of the audience. And the basic cure is to see oneself Home and live here facelessly, live from within outwards, live to express not impress. What people make of one then is their business: one's own business is one's Void – and the people who fill It. To strike them as a real, sincere, natural, game-free person, it is only necessary to attend to the Nothing here and leave all such build-up – one's development from this Empty Source here to its regional effects in them – to take care of itself. To be interested in one's self-image is to spoil it. Deliberately to project a self is to project a false self. While seeing Who one really is, one is game-free; while overlooking This, one is at least playing the Face Game, and probably some of its derivatives as well.

One finds peace of mind. At the Centre is always perfection, off-Centre always imperfection. Man as man is (to say the least) lacking, and no amount of seeing Who he really is will make a human into an angel or the human scene into Utopia, let alone Heaven. The effects of his seeing will, if he persists, certainly become evident in his personality and environment, but they will vary immensely and will often seem to him to be very meagre indeed. One thing alone can be relied on through all circumstances, and that is their Core of Peace. The seer may often find himself in a tragic and sad and puzzling and troublesome world, but he never (so long as he's seeing) lacks peace of mind. His basic anxiety has gone. Seeing that he is indeed Peace Itself, he is at rest.

COURSE COMMENTS

Your experiment with the mirror reminded me of when I was a little girl, not sure what age, maybe 8 years or so. But I remember living from what I now have the word to describe as consciousness. I was experiencing life from the fullest with no limits, until one day I looked in the mirror and saw my face, and realized that I was looking at what other's saw. I felt disappointed, because I had been living as though I was already beautiful, until I looked that day at my reflection. It then made me feel self-conscious, comparing myself to others' faces that I saw. I saw that I was different. (I appeared just kinda plain, where I saw others as beautiful.) It was literally the day that changed my life and how I interacted with others.

Janet

By doing the homework of pointing at different things during the day and then back at yourself again it becomes more and more clear what you mean. The nothingness is there but at the same time it is the universe. 'Wow' is the right statement to make about that.

Anne-Marie

Thank you very much for your efforts, I think these classes are magnificent. After a couple of years of searching the spiritual world for the truth about my Self I can say now that I can retire.

Anthony

———

This is one of the most beautiful realizations I have become aware of. I cannot thank you enough for your sharing.

Bryan

———

When I first read about the experiments I literally couldn't believe what I 'saw', so I sat down one evening by myself and decided that I would 'find' the core of myself. I sat down and tried. And tried, and tried, and tried. The more I tried the more frustrated I became, and eventually gave up, feeling that I had failed. I woke up early the next morning and almost laughed out loud! Of course I had not failed. In fact, I had unwittingly proved the truth of Douglas's teachings to my little self. Amazing!

Mara

HOMEWORK

- Whenever you remember, notice you are face to no-face with others.
- Do the Tube experiment with a friend.
- Every so often, point at your no-face and take a few moments to look into this special place.

CHAPTER FIVE

RESISTANCE

When we identify only with what we look like, we see ourselves as mortal. When we see what we really are, we discover our true Self is immortal. What a wonderful discovery.

So why don't we all say Yes! to our true Self?

Everyone tells me *I am what I look like*. Who am I to disagree? Especially because I want to belong - I want to be part of society. (I need to be accepted.) Won't I be ostracised if I talk about being headless? (I don't find many others admitting it.) Won't people think I'm deluded if I say the world is within me? (I can't cope with strange looks.) Or they will say I'm foolish. (I've had enough of being laughed at!) Anyway, it's heresy to say you are God. (Unacceptable.) For many of us this kind of social pressure puts us off.

Another difficulty is that who we really are takes on the pain and suffering of the world as well as its joy. Yes it's wonderful being capacity for the scent of a flower, a star shining in the night sky, a piece of music we love. These things are easy to embrace. How lovely to be faceless for the face of a child, laughing and giggling! But the suffering of the world around us? The suffering of the people close to us? Our own suffering? This is not so easy. Understandably, we draw lines to protect ourselves.

But perhaps all our resistance to our true Self boils down to one fear: the fear of death. Seeing is a kind of death – in fact it is the deepest of all deaths. When you step over the line above your chest, you step into complete non-existence. Nothing of you remains.

The paradox is that when we die this deepest of deaths, we are in the same moment born into the widest of lives. When we cross this frontier at the edge of our world, death does not follow. What does follow is endless life. Being. What threatened to be the most dangerous place, this yawning abyss, turns out to be the safest. Here we are secure, no matter what is happening there - nothing can harm our true Self. Our fear and resistance have no real foundation.

— EXPERIMENT 8 —

Resistance and Surrender

Things resist other things, but no-thing resists nothing – our true Self welcomes everything. Let's see if this is true.

Put your hands together and gently push them against each other. Each resists the other. Neither moves. You feel pressure and discomfort.

Now let one of them yield so that it gives way to the other. The pressure disappears and there's movement. One hand surrenders to the force of the other.

Repeat the experiment but this time notice you are observing your two opposing hands from aware nothingness.

Does this nothingness side with one hand over the other? Does it object either to their conflict, or to the yielding of one to the other? How could it? Nothing does not resist or object to anything happening, nor does it choose one thing over another. It welcomes everything.

Do the experiment again, each hand pushing against the other, but this time, instead of then letting one hand push the other, move them away from each other. Neither 'wins' nor 'loses'. Does the nothingness prefer this outcome? How can nothingness have preferences?

There in the region of things you resist or yield; here in the region of nothing you always yield. There in the region of things you have preferences, you choose this or that; here in the region of no-thing you have no preferences, you accept everything. You say Yes! to things just as they are.

TRUST

Accepting things as they are is accepting things as they flow from the Source, from your innermost being. Whilst my true Self accepts all that happens, as Richard sometimes I accept, sometimes I resist.

Usually there is a process whereby I start by resisting something I don't like, then gradually my resistance melts (as perhaps I begin realising I cannot change what is happening), until finally I accept, at first grudgingly but in the end whole-heartedly (I hope!). As I begin yielding to what is happening often I discover unforeseen benefits emerging in the situation. (Meanwhile my true Self remains unconditionally open to whatever is happening, including my resistance.)

Here's an example: After I began revising these paragraphs about resistance and trust, I found myself running short of writing time. I had agreed to go away for a few days (to do a job of work, combined with visiting friends in the same area) and the day when I had to leave was fast approaching. I began wishing I hadn't accepted the job. 'If only I was staying at home, then I could carry on writing. Now I'm going to have to interrupt my writing, and I'm going to have to drive a long way.' (It was a five hour journey.) 'I'm not looking forward to this at all.' When the day arrived I set off, feeling resistant and annoyed with myself. After about three hours driving I began accepting there was no turning back. Slowly I began yielding to the situation. And as I yielded my feelings changed. The further I drove the more open I became to what was happening – the landscape flowing through this stillness, the music I was listening to, the reflections about my life now possible since I was no longer absorbed in my writing… By the time I met my friends I had forgotten my resistance and was enjoying being away from home.

I discovered that my friend Camilla was going to be in London a few days later. Camilla and I had first shared Seeing in 1970 when I was 17 and she was 12. Then in 1997 she and her boyfriend Jon were kidnapped in Chechnya and held hostage for 14 months. The idea occurred to me that I could interview her on camera about how Seeing had helped her cope with this ordeal. She agreed, visited me in London a few days later, we recorded the interview and I put it on Youtube. Through this film she has inspired many people. Looking back, I realise the interview happened because I had accepted that job! The job led me to Camilla's and then to the idea of an interview. And, following this interview, I have started doing other ones with other friends. It is a good way of showing how Seeing works in different people's lives. In spite of my doubts and resistance, I now see that the One I really am had organised things well. (I don't think it knew what it was doing beforehand. As Kierkegaard said, 'Life is lived forwards and understood backwards'.)

I hadn't begun trusting the One (in other words, I hadn't begun losing my resistance!) until about half-way to Camilla's. Yet even while I was resisting I was aware that my true Self was unconditionally accepting all that was happening, including my resistance. I would even say that although I wasn't trusting the One, I could see that it was trusting itself, that it was welcoming without reservation all that was happening, simply because it is built that way - it is built unconditionally open. Or, put in yet another way - on the surface I doubt, but deep down I am confident. And, ironically, during this short period away from my writing, I learned more about what I was writing about - resistance and trust – and am now drawing inspiration from that experience!

A Reason for Trusting

Why should I trust the One? How do I know it will give me what I need? I don't. There's no guarantee. Trusting the One is an experiment, a leap of faith. However, consider who the One is. The One has achieved being. No one can explain how the One did this – or rather, how the One is achieving being *here and now*. Even the One doesn't know how it does this - I know that the One doesn't know because I am the One and, looking within, I find no explanation. I am a mystery. My puzzlement and astonishment at the mystery and miracle of the One's existence is the One's own puzzlement and astonishment. How do I create myself? I have no idea.

My astonishment is coupled with praise and adoration: how clever the One is to create itself - how inventive, imaginative, powerful, generous, merciful…

If I can't trust this One, who can I trust?

The One does not always give me what I want. When I resist what it gives me, I suffer. When I accept, I am at peace. Looking within, I find the place that always accepts, that is always at peace - that is peace.

The Scent Of Daffodils

Richard Lang

The soul that is attached to anything, however much good there may be in it, will not arrive at the liberty of divine union.

ST. JOHN OF THE CROSS (1542 – 91)

One autumn I bought two large bags of daffodils. I planted them at the beginning of December, which is late in the year to plant bulbs. Most of them I put in the garden but some I placed in two long deep trays and in February I brought these inside. I was hoping the warmth of the kitchen would bring them out early. Soon daffodil shoots were racing upwards, sharp like green spears. Such powerful thrusting, such thirst for life! And so many of them! A glorious display was surely in the making.

And yet, even before their buds had appeared I was fearing their demise, afraid they would be gone before I had really taken them in. I wanted to slow down their growth, mentally photographing them so that I might always see them. Conscious of time passing I was not heeding Blake's words:

He who binds to himself a joy
Does the wingéd life destroy;
But he who kisses the joy as it flies
Lives in eternity's sunrise.

Suddenly buds were appearing. Then buds were opening. I welcomed their explosion into my life. I moved a tray to the living room and placed it on the low chest of drawers that stands in front of the huge gilt-edged mirror on the wall. So many buds were now opening each day I could barely keep pace! Reflected in the mirror, fifty flowers were now a hundred - luscious green leaves and bold yellow blossoms reaching out in every direction, uninhibited, shouting their existence, a wild party in full swing. Intoxicating scent filled the room.

One afternoon I was admiring their beauty when I became more conscious of my desire to possess them. Gazing at their open innocent faces and breathing in their strong perfume, I just couldn't get enough. Greedy, I didn't even want to look away in case I missed something! My eyes wanted to drink them in and in, my nose wanted to smell their scent over and over. And even though their buds had only just opened I was dreading the moment I would notice the flowers fading. I kept checking for the first signs of jaded petals, of precious freshness passing. Aware of their short lives I found myself wishing for eternal spring. My heart ached, conscious of the fleeting nature of life.

The next morning, lying in the bath, I was thinking about how possessive I felt towards those daffodils. I wanted them to stay there, in full bloom, forever. I wanted to have them, own them, control them, preserve them in amber!

Then an obvious, perennial truth came home to me again. Really I can possess nothing. Everything comes and goes, slipping like sand through my fingers, vanishing like smoke in the wind. These flowers are independent of me.

They have their own life. I don't own them and can never own them. I water them and provide them with light and soil, but I lack the power to make them stay. I can only witness their momentary beauty. Then they are gone.

Yet this wasn't the whole story. Something else stirred in me. Alongside my feelings of powerlessness and – well, my fear of death – I experienced the presence of a mystery that survives the passing of things. I awoke to my innermost being. Just when I am struggling, hoping against hope that I can hold on to something precious, I stumble again upon that which I can never lose. I stumble upon that which I am, the one thing I do possess. It may sound strange to say I possess this – this which is indefinable, ungraspable, belonging to no one, dissolving all me-ness. Do I possess it or does it possess me? I don't know. Yet today I feel it is mine. Mine because I am it, through and through. Nothing can ever separate me from this.

And so I am this emptiness - the bare, plain, scentless void.

And yet, how lovely. Today the void that I am smells of fresh daffodils!

———

Where I'm coming from is upstream of life. It is the source of life, yes, but it is not alive. From Here I look out upon a snail or the daffodil there, let alone you, and, my God, I discover life.

DOUGLAS HARDING

———

— EXPERIMENT 9 —

Stress to No Stress

Look at your hand. You are observing it from emptiness. This is two-way looking – thing there seen from no-thing here, colour there seen in clearness here, shape there presented to the absence of shape here. Now tense your hand into a fist. You feel stress there, arising in the absence of stress here. Now relax your hand. The tension melts away – a relaxed feeling takes its place in the unchanging absence of feeling here.

Here at centre you are always free of stress. There, in your body, in your mind, in your world, there may be at times lots of stress. Always there will be some – life is like that. The key to peace and health is seeing that you operate in this stressful world from this stress-free space.

Draw on this resource whenever you find yourself in a stressful situation. Stay aware of the stress-free space here whilst remaining aware of whatever stress you are experiencing there.

This stress-free emptiness isn't a special state of mind created or maintained by a technique – it is the stress-free emptiness in which all states of mind come and go. This full emptiness is always available, whatever your mood, whatever your situation.

Your body and mind get stressed, but your true Self is always at ease.

— EXPERIMENT 10 —

Spinning the World

Rushing about in our daily lives, we yearn to be still. But as soon as we are still, we get bored and want to be on the move. We are difficult to please. Yet we can have the best of both worlds – we can be still and moving *at the same time*.

If I stand up and turn round on the spot, you see me turning whilst the room stays still.

But from my point of view I remain still whilst the room turns.

Try it. Stand up, point at your no-face and carefully turn round. What moves? Beyond your finger, the room moves past. Is there any movement on your side of your finger? Don't you remain still?

Sometimes I experiment turning round for a few minutes. (If you try this, make sure you are safe. Stop if you get dizzy.) As the room flows past I relax into the stillness where I am. There's nowhere to go, nothing to do. It is as if the stillness gets deeper, more solid. Breathing out, I let go of being anything or anyone. As well as being profound, it's fun. I remember as a child making the world dance like this – before I learned to edit out the dance and see myself as others saw me, on the move in a still world.

Alternatively, go for a walk and notice that you remain still whilst the scenery flows through you. Or when you are driving, observe that you go nowhere whilst your destination comes to you. It's the only way to travel!

Our seemingly irreconcilable needs for movement and rest are reconciled.

The Qutb (Pole) is he who turns round himself; round him is the revolution of the heavenly spheres.

RUMI

~~~~~~~~~~

As we rush, as we rush in the Train,
The trees and the houses go wheeling back,
But the starry heavens above the plain
Come flying on our track.

JAMES THOMSON

~~~~~~~~~~

Why do you think that you are active? Take the gross example of your arrival here. You left home in a cart, took a train, alighted at the railway station here, got into a cart there and found yourself in this Ashram. When asked, you say you travelled all the way here from your town. Is it true? Is it not a fact that you remained as you were and there were movements... all along the way? Just as those movements are confounded with your own, so also the other activities. They are not your own.

RAMANA MAHARSHI

~~~~~~~~~~

When I cross the bridge, it is the bridge that flows, not the water.

ZEN SAYING

~~~~~~~~~~

The outward man is the swinging door; the inner man is the still hinge.

MEISTER ECKHART

~~~~~~~~~~

The only thing moved is matter.

PLOTINUS

~~~~~~~~~~

Whoever says that the Tathagata goes or comes, sits or lies down, he does not understand the meaning of my teaching.

DIAMOND SUTRA

~~~~~~~~~~

At the centre, where no-one abides, there this light is quenched... for this Ground is the impartible stillness, motionless in itself, and by this Immobility all things are moved.

MEISTER ECKHART

~~~~~~~~~~

And every Space that a man views around his dwelling-place
Standing on his own roof or in his garden on a mount
Of twenty-five cubits in height, such space is his Universe:
And on its verge the Sun rises and sets, the Clouds bow
To meet the flat Earth and the Sea in such an order'd Space:
The Starry heavens reach no further, but here bend and set
On all sides, and the two Poles turn on their valves of gold;
And if he move his dwelling-place, his heavens also move
Where'er he goes, and all his neighbourhood bewail his loss.
Such are the Spaces called Earth and such its dimension.

WILLIAM BLAKE

COURSE COMMENTS

It was interesting to come home tonight and find the lesson about the putting on of faces. I've been at a supervision group for psychotherapists tonight where we were engaging very directly in reflecting each other's faces and allowing space to speak – very useful and powerful.

────

Yes, I'm very doubtful. Got some hints of something, but I just can't literally see it yet. I can understand it, but I can't see it in that really simple way people do.

The 'common sense' image is just too strong!

———

One of the aspects I find interesting about the headless way is its immediate impact – the basic experience of headlessness feels very accessible. I wonder if there is an issue about how people go on to work with it and how easy that is. I came across Douglas Harding's work about 19 years ago... The experience was completely clear and not a little freaky but somewhere it wasn't right for me to pursue it at that time, and I have come to this much later after experiencing a revolution in awareness.

———

I find looking from the first person to be really effective in reminding me how things are and being very simple about it. Driving down the M4 motorway today, watching it rush towards and through me, and just now seeing my hands moving across the keys and noticing that at a certain point in the field of vision there simply is nothing there.
The mirror experiment makes so much sense that I'm sitting here kind of stunned. It's something that I've always said, but never really believed. That we're not the person we're looking at, that what we're looking at is simply a facade for our true being.

———

I have a sort of different view on the headless body. For years I have been questioning the idea of outer beauty. Here it is, this face that belongs to you, that you spend time beautifying when in all actuality it belongs to everyone else, everyone else who sees it during your life. So how can it belong to you when it belongs to everyone else? Just curious.

Heather

———

Many thanks for these classes – first time I have used this kind of resource and I'm finding it fascinating and a very convenient way to try to understand. What I do feel I can get to grips with is the "me as empty space" part. I view it like this:
There is an empty box on the table – but when I look inside, it is not actually empty, it's full of space. This fullness can take on other aspects depending on what is put into it. I put a clock in and the box has the ability to be a timekeeper; I add a bell and when moved the box has the ability to make music; I add a lavender bag and the box has the ability to scent the room. But as all this happens, the 'box' is still a box – it's just a 'vehicle' for all the stuff that can take place in the fullness of space.
The box's space is finite. My space is not. I can add indefinitely to my space – the more I grow the more it grows and I never become a timekeeper, though

I wear a watch; a musical instrument, though I wear a bell. I just increase my capacity by adding to it.

Helen

_____

I am taking the class and have found it most interesting. I have shared some of the experiments with a close friend. We went to the river Sunday and experienced no-head as we looked out at all that is. I have for a while accepted the concept of Oneness with all. These experiments validate what I have understood. I have found that when I choose to be head-less the actions of others do not have the impact on my emotions that they do when I choose to be a limited person. I am interested to continue this and see the wonder of growing and sharing with all of you.

Donna

_____

Thank you very much for the course, which I am finding very useful and important indeed. I have experienced a steady growth in my understanding and ability to notice my headlessness and that the various descriptions in the exercises in fact describe reality very accurately, despite being at odds with conventional wisdom. The result is often a profound sense of peace, lightness and brightness of my perception combined with a subtle sense of being at one with my surroundings. I find myself losing this sense quite often, especially when confronted, as I often am in my job, with situations which require thinking out solutions and dealing with tense interpersonal situations. Here too however, I found the exercise about stress quite helpful. All in all I am finding all this very helpful and valuable.

Michael

_____

You offer understanding at a level that anyone can become truly enlightened to who they are and move forward in love and compassion.

Sandy

_____

I am fascinated. I came to Douglas's teaching via the website a few months ago, and immediately 'saw' that there is nothing above my shoulders! This class is reinforcing and amplifying this amazing revelation. Thank you for teaching it.

Mara

_____

This discovery truly is not just for a chosen few. It is for anyone willing and interested enough to LOOK and check it out 1st person/1st hand!

Karen

————

In your reply you seem to imply that for you the 1st-person position is reasonably constant, obviously practised over a number of years. For someone beginning to open to this disposition there are so many things that are just taken for granted. I am assuming then that everything is to be questioned, everything must be seen from the 1st-person point of view. In that way the difference would then become obvious, right? To put it very simply then, the practice is to persist in seeing from the 1st person until it eventually becomes constant. Is that right?

Steve

————

Thank you very much for the enlightening course! Since my conditioning of the 3rd personhood is so strong, the only thing I could do is to add noticing my headlessness to the old perspective and wait for the transformation to happen. I am certain that something already experienced in childhood must be more natural in its true sense than something learned through social conditioning, even though the unlearning process seems harder than just 'seeing' innocently at this moment.

Headlessly yours, Kiyohiko

————

My husband did the first session with me, and he was amazed that through the experiments he was able, for the first time in his life, to actually separate his awareness from his physical body! It's as if awareness is 'contagious'.

Deb

Social Results

Douglas Harding, from *The Toolkit for Testing the Incredible Hypothesis*

The Disease

It is clear that our great social ills spring from greed and hate; and our hypothesis implies (with, as we have seen, good reason) that these in turn spring from delusion – delusion as to What and Who we are. If we let ourselves be conned into believing we really are what we look like *to others*, mere 3rd persons plural, then we are sure to suffer from feelings of inadequacy, insecurity, meaninglessness, loneliness, alienation, resentment, self-pity, fear, and profound anxiety –

and of course to behave accordingly. All these are symptoms of one disease, one madness – the madness of mistaking absolutely one's own identity. A man who is sure he is a teapot, or Napoleon, or a ball of glass, we feel sorry for; but a man who is sure he is a man - and nothing else – is in fact no less crazy, and no less to be pitied. Seeing himself as a mere thing among things, he is wandering, out of his Mind, eccentric, far gone – a wool-gathering member of a society intent on distracting his attention from the Spot he occupies, from the Centre he lives from, from the Being he is.

It wouldn't be quite so bad if he knew *which* thing to be. Unable to reconcile different observers' pictures of himself, or to decide which of them to take on for this and that occasion, which mask to wear, and which role to play, he goes crazier still. His only cure is to *un*thing himself. About each man there are as many views as viewers, and all of them different; about the No-thing they are all gathered around, only one.

The Therapy

To come to his senses he has to turn round and see What he is *to himself*. This is the only lasting and radical psychotherapy – for the patient to discover (and go on re-discovering) Who the patient is. This alone is sanity, to stop pretending one is somebody else. Being whole is being 1st person, because being 1st person is being the Whole.

It all comes back, inevitably, to the individual – to the individual as 1st person singular, present tense:-

If I see that here, whether I like it or not, I'm built for letting you in, for love, how can I go on trying to shut you out? If I see that my 1st person Core coincides and merges absolutely with yours, how could I go on trying to score over you and put you down, to rob or cheat or injure you in any way? I should only be hurting myself.

If already I embrace and contain the world, why should I go on clutching at these insignificant little bits of it – these possessions which possess me rather than I them – so frantically?

If, faceless here, I gratefully take on your face, so that it is now more mine than mine is, how can I object to its colour or cast or features? Who, when white confronts black, has the black face?

If I find that, by living the 1st person life, I get all the satisfactions (real or hoped-for) of drug-use safely and more surely, then what is the point of continuing to rely on drugs, or to use them at all?

If I learn to prize instead of to fear the Emptiness here, why should I go on trying to fill it by over-eating, tippling, smoking (on a radio programme about cigarette addiction, two speakers agreed they smoked 'to fill the empty space between their ears'); or by making-up, fidgeting with glasses, chin-stroking and hair-patting, grimacing, non-stop chatter – as if to persuade myself there must be *something* here to stick this great big pipe in, to dab all this powder and lipstick on, to fuss and fiddle with? As if to persuade myself there *must* be a head here, with a hole in it for stuffing all these alien substances into? As if to persuade myself there *must* be some kind of loud-speaker here, to make all this noise?

And so on. In general, *seeing What one's behaviour is coming out of, seeing Whose it is, is bound to affect that behaviour radically.* The evidence available amply confirms this. And the social effects of this in-seeing, this interior revolution, this turn-about of a growing number of individuals, are probably far greater than they suspect.

The Future

The question is: what are the chances of enough people seeing clearly enough What and Who they are, and doing so quickly enough to change our ailing society in time to save it? For the following reasons, the chances aren't as small as they might seem:

Youth. Among intelligent young people all over the world, interest in matters linked with our hypothesis – in meditation, mystical experience, and altered states of consciousness – is quickly gaining ground, and the future lies with their generation. Certainly there is overwhelming evidence that, unlike so many of their elders, they see their faceless Identity very easily, and that a sizeable proportion are coming to value it. (Very often, of course, the seeing isn't followed up by the meditation we have described. But all isn't lost. Once having been seen clearly in youth, It can always be re-seen in later life, when the need for basic therapy is becoming more and more painfully evident. This isn't a skill which one is liable, by neglect, altogether to lose the knack of.)

Communications. The ever-growing means and speed and spread of communications make it possible for a useful discovery, catching on here today, to be everywhere tomorrow.

The power of an idea. History, the underlying assumptions of a society, the manifest climate of opinion – in any case these aren't changed by vast numbers of people acting in concert. It is always an influential minority, sometimes a very small one, which leads the way. And what governs history, beneath all the show of physical power, is the power of ideas, and specially "the power of an idea whose time has come"; and more specially (we may hopefully add) the power of something suddenly *seen* to be true, having previously been overlooked by the majority of mankind.

Children as teachers. If such an idea can get going in the schools, it is well on the way. At the pupil's level, of course, 1st-personhood (which is the actualisation of our hypothesis) lies at, or just under, the surface. Children don't *need* our Toolkit, but do enjoy it, and many see the point of its tests and exercises at once. (How long will it be before a school has one classroom – the children's very own – dedicated to *un*schooling and *un*knowing, to seeing oneself as one sees oneself, and seeing the world as one sees the world, instead of seeing what one is taught to see: a class in which the children themselves prove and enjoy the hypothesis which parents and teachers and society in general are so determined to make incredible?)

Who, anyway, sees the Point? In the last resort, the spreading of our hypothesis isn't a matter of counting heads but counting No-heads – and the answer is One. After all, when I see What's here, it isn't a case of a man (as such), one of thousands of millions, who is seeing This, but of This seeing itself in me – *in* this man but not *as* this man. No individual's Enlightenment can be contained; it must spill over because it *is*, in truth, the Enlightenment of all. Therefore it follows that the social influence (deep, hidden, but perhaps all the wider and stronger for that) of just one unknown but dedicated seer could be decisive for the world's future.

For if our hypothesis is true, isn't it what the Universe is all about? If the purpose of the One's seeming Self-division into you and me and the others is its own heightened Self-consciousness in us, the joy of Self-recognition, then hasn't this marvellous goal been partly won already? Isn't our own experience of this joy our evidence? Can we believe this to be the end of the story? Has the One shot Its bolt, come to the end of Its ingenuity, exhausted Its energies, got bored with re-discovering Itself? Merely to put such questions is, surely, to take heart. Can anyone who is seriously trying out our hypothesis remain a pessimist – even about human society?

The Three Stages of Man's Development

We have distinguished three stages of development: (1) the virtual and unconscious 1st-personhood of infancy, when our hypothesis is lived, (2) the conscious 3rd-personhood of the unenlightened adult, when our hypothesis is denied, and (3) the actual and conscious 1st-personhood of the enlightened adult, when our hypothesis becomes self-evident truth – without denial of 3rd-personhood.

The implications for the future of education are that it should tolerate and even encourage in the child an unbroken thread of 1st-personhood, running through and counterbalancing the necessary (but at present so often disastrous) acquisition of 3rd-personhood: and our observations confirm that this thread (however thin it may wear, and need to wear) need not be broken: shades of the prison-house *don't* have to close impenetrably upon the growing boy – or girl. It *is* possible to find one's face without losing one's No-face.

And the implications for the future of the race are that those fortunate children who are already coming through the educational machine without total loss of Identity – of their luminous Core, their at-largeness – plus those fortunate adults who are re-discovering theirs, are taking the next step in evolution. Ahead of their time, they lead the way to a society in which the Self-consciousness of the 1st person will be as normal (which isn't to say as common) as the self-consciousness of the 3rd person is now.

HOMEWORK

- Go for a walk and watch the scenery move. Be the still space through which everything flows.
- Don't move an inch when you're driving! Let the streets and countryside do all the work!
- Be still and let the world dance – be the dance.
- Next time you are in a stressful situation, notice it is stress there, no-stress here. Keep returning to this stress-free place - the place you have never left.

CHAPTER SIX

MORE DIFFICULTIES

Some people (on the internet course) said they couldn't see their *nothingness*. If you are thinking this, you may be under the impression that you're meant to see a nothingness that exists separately from the world, a kind of black hole all on its own. It's not like this – at least, it's not like this for me. I do not experience this headless space existing all alone, without things in it. To me, that's an idea of emptiness, not my experience of it. This headless space is never just empty, never separate from the world. I look, notice I do not see my head, and *at the same time* see the world instead of my head.

Someone else said he couldn't *understand* 'nothingness'. Nor can I! Things can be explained (to a degree), but the nothing-that-is-everything is in a league of its own – it cannot be explained. We cannot say where it came from, or how it came to be. Fortunately we don't have to understand it to see it. Though it's a mystery, it's accessible – visible, audible, tangible.

TOUCHING YOUR HEAD

Another objection people raise is that they can see their *noses* and *feel* their heads. The following extract from *On Having No Head* looks into this.

Making Sense Of The Seeing

Douglas Harding

My first objection was: my head may be missing, but not its nose. Here it is, visibly preceding me wherever I go. And my answer was: if this fuzzy, pinkish, yet perfectly transparent cloud suspended on my right, and this other similar cloud suspended on my left, are noses, then I count two of them and not one; and the perfectly opaque single protuberance which I observe so clearly in the middle of your face is not a nose: only a hopelessly dishonest or confused observer would deliberately use the same name for such utterly different things. I prefer to go by my dictionary and common usage, which oblige me to say that, whereas nearly all human beings have a nose apiece, I have none.

All the same, if some misguided sceptic, over-anxious to make his point, were to strike out in this direction, aiming mid-way between these two pink clouds, the result would surely be as unpleasant as if I owned the most solid and punchable of noses. Again, what about this complex of subtle tensions, movements, pressures, itches, tickles, aches, warmths, and throbbings, never entirely absent from this central region? Above all, what about these touch-feelings which arise when I explore here with my hand? Surely these findings add up to massive evidence for the existence of my head right here and now after all?

I find they do nothing of the sort. No doubt a great variety of sensations are plainly given here and cannot be ignored, but they don't amount to a head, or anything like one. The only way to make a head out of them would be to throw in all sorts of ingredients that are plainly missing here – in particular, all manner of coloured shapes in three dimensions. What sort of head is it that, though containing innumerable sensations, is observed to lack eyes, ears, mouth, hair, and indeed all the bodily equipment which other heads are observed to contain? The plain fact is that this place must be kept clear of all such obstructions, of the slightest mistiness or colouring which could cloud my universe.

In any case, when I start groping around for my lost head, instead of finding it here I only lose my exploring hand as well: it, too, is swallowed up in the abyss at the centre of my being. Apparently this yawning cavern, this unoccupied base of all my operations, this nearest but virtually unknown region, this magical locality where I thought I kept my head, is in fact more like a beacon-fire so fierce that all things approaching it are instantly and utterly consumed, in order that its world-illuminating brilliance and clarity shall never for a moment be obscured. As for these lurking aches and tickles and so on, they can no more quench or shade this central brightness than these mountains and clouds and sky can do so. Quite the contrary: they all exist in its shining, and through them it is seen to shine. Present experience, whatever sense is employed, occurs only in an empty and absent head. For here and now my world and my head are incompatibles: they won't mix. There is no room for both at once on these shoulders, and fortunately it is my head with all its anatomy that has to go. This is not a matter of argument, or of philosophical acumen, or of working oneself up into a state, but of simple sight – of LOOK-WHO'S-HERE instead of IMAGINE-WHO'S-HERE, instead of TAKE-EVERYBODY-ELSE'S-WORD-FOR-WHO'S-HERE. If I fail to see what I am (and especially what I am not) it's because I'm too busily imaginative, too 'spiritual', too adult and knowing, too credulous, too intimidated by society and language, too frightened of the obvious to accept the situation exactly as I find it at this moment. Only I am in a position to report on what's here. A kind of alert naivety is what I need. It takes an innocent eye and an empty head (not to mention a stout heart) to admit their own perfect emptiness.

—EXPERIMENT 11—

Touching your No-Head

Hold your hands out in front of you.

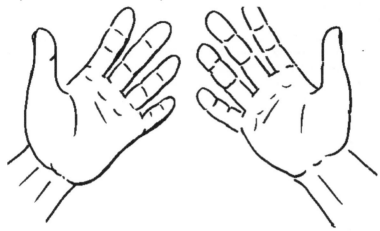

Move them towards you and touch your head. You feel something. Does this 'something' have a colour or a shape? How big is it? How solid? Is it a 'thing'?

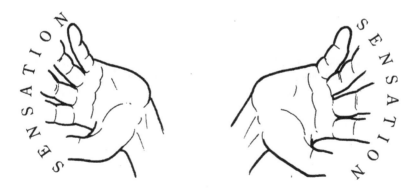

Do the sensations you feel occur on the surface of your head, or in boundless, awake emptiness? Go by present evidence, not by what you assume is true. Are you touching your head, or your no-head?

My sensations are in the awake emptiness I'm looking out of, just as everything is in this awake emptiness.

Hold your ears. How wide apart are those sensations? As wide as the world? Look at those hands disappearing – disappearing into what?

Of course I've learned to connect these invisible sensations to the head I see in the mirror - I see my hands touching my head there in the mirror and imagine they are touching the same thing here. But I don't *see* my hands touching my head *here* – I see them disappearing. From my point of view, all these sensations are happening in space here. This is a case of trusting my experience rather than automatically accepting what I am told, even though what I find is the opposite of what society tells me.

Of course, to see the world I need my head, my eyes, my brain, and the cells, molecules and particles they are made of, but I am not seeing *from* these layers - I see with and through them *from my centre* - from this self-evidently aware *space*. It is not Richard but the One within Richard that is aware. In reality, only God sees the stars – or hears the wind, or greets a friend…

―――――――――――

If sense-data are literally inside the brain we are committed to the conclusion that they are always smaller than the things to which they belong, [or else] that our own head is very much larger than it appears to be from touch.

H. H. PRICE

~~~~~~~~~~~~

The aspects of things that are most important for us are hidden because of their simplicity and familiarity… We fail to be struck by what, once seen, is most striking and most powerful.

LUDWIG WITTGENSTEIN

~~~~~~~~~~~~

The average person, while he thinks he is awake, actually is half asleep. By 'half asleep' I mean that his contact with reality is a very partial one; most of what he believes to be reality (outside or inside of himself) is a set of fictions which his mind constructs. He is aware of reality only to the degree to which his social functioning makes it necessary.

ERICH FROMM

~~~~~~~~~~~~

I believe I see – but I only see words; I believe I feel, but I only think feelings. The cerebrating person is the alienated person.

ERICH FROMM

~~~~~~~~~~~~

We should be as very strangers to the thoughts, customs, and opinions of men in the world, as if we were but little children. So those things would appear to us only which do to children when they are first born.

THOMAS TRAHERNE

The Sage all the time sees and hears no more than an infant sees and hears.

LAO-TZU

~~~~~~~~~~~~

Observe things as they are and don't pay attention to other people.

HUANG-PO

COURSE COMMENTS

I must tell you about the haircut I've just had. Andy did it. At times Andy's hand and scissors disappeared into the Void here; then his whole arm; then both hands and his head. Several times his whole body went, leaving only his voice. And sometimes not even leaving that. Then he would appear again, perhaps without a hand and without scissors. Finally he became smaller and stood making satisfied expressions. Never has having a haircut been so enjoyable or so enlightening.

Roger

I like the emphasis on looking only at what is there and not at what I imagine to be there, such as noticing that the image in the mirror is in the mirror without mentally pasting it on myself and wearing it. I've also noticed that it is much easier to be in contact with the void when I am alone, and that taking time to being alone each day is essential. This is obvious, but it seems as if the most obvious things are what we usually overlook, like the fact that we have never even seen our own head!

The more I continue with this course, the more and more I am amazed at how simple 'being' is. I feel more in tune with the world than I have been in a long time, and happier too. And my hope is that this happiness will be absorbed by everyone out 'there' - who is also part of me, within me.

The sightless experiment is something I loved to do even as a child. I have always been good at navigating in the dark and doing things blindfolded, and the whole experiment of listening to the silence was wonderful... hearing cars come and go (I live off a busy highway), planes overhead, the soft hum of the computer, the sound of the air conditioner as it turned itself on and off, voices of people walking past on the pavement... I must have sat there for a good half hour just listening and re-experiencing what it was like as a child to do this.

I'm sure my husband thought me a little silly again as I was staring at him while he was reading. And as I read what you had written, how we exchange faces, I find myself with a new way of seeing people. Long have I been aware of energy exchange as described in *The Celestine Prophecy* by James Redfield, but this is something quite unique. To be able to give your 'headlessness' to someone in the form of my face, and take theirs in exchange... it's quite awesome. To me, I don't think I'll look at another person the same again. I am giving a part of me to them, and taking a part of them in me. I am trusting them with 'me' and sharing my energy with them too, and I realise at the same time that we are all one. I feel pain and they feel pain. I feel joy and joy is theirs. I would like to show the world more joy and happiness because the world has enough pain. I'm not sure if this makes sense or not, but it does to me so I guess that's what matters. I just found these experiments wonderful and life-changing.

Donna

———

I am very impressed by what I've already read... and tried. Until yesterday I had no time to read the classes I've already received, so I'm a little bit delayed. :) Nonetheless I've succeeded in 'seeing into Nothingness', and I'm deeply moved. Thank you, Richard, with all my heart.

———

Yesterday I was in an airplane. Putting my face against the window, I saw a huge expanse of sky and ocean. If someone were looking into that window from outside, they would have seen my face pressed against the glass. But looking into myself as I looked out, I saw no face and no airplane. In fact I saw nothing at all. This no-thing is always ample enough to accommodate whatever shows up. Right now it contains a TV monitor and a small room.

———

I did some of the Headless exercises (pointing forward and back, clenched fist and fingers stroking palm), and invented a new one: Thumbing My Nose. Hold your fist in front of your face and stick your thumb straight, but gently against your nose, and move it slightly. Feel your nose, your thumb. See the nose image extending momentarily and freshly within awareness. Shift into allowing awareness of awareness to be primary. Consider the deep inner meaning of the common social signal of thumbing your nose: 'You can't bug me... You're just an image in my own awareness... I cannot be victim, for I am master within my own awareness.' I find fresh awakenings happening yesterday and today, easily and surprisingly, like baths in void, with tinges of joy. I've sent Classes 1 and 3 to over 50 friends and awareness teachers.

Richard

———

Personal Relationships

1977 interview with Douglas Harding

Richard: Would you say that seeing Who you are improves personal relationships?

Douglas: I am sure of it, to be absolutely honest. I mean, I know that we tend to be very careful of making claims for the advantages and results of seeing Who one is, but yes, I would say that seeing Who you are not only improves personal relationships but in a certain sense is the indispensable basis for good personal relationship. Because what is personal relationship in the Seeing sense? It is not relationship at all. It is an asymmetrical situation when I am empty for you and I am not putting anything in your way and I am open for and I am you. I am your essence and I have your face. This is personal relationship, the only personal relationship which works. It is not a personal relationship really, it is identity. I think this is built into the Seeing experience. So it is not a case of improving personal relationships, it is in a certain sense superseding them or getting to their basis.

Richard: If one feels that one isn't loving enough, what light does seeing Who you are shed on that problem?

Douglas: Well, I think that it sheds an enormous light. Seeing is not concerned with feeling, it is concerned with fact. And if I see Who I am I find that my very nature is openness. In a certain non-sentimental, non-feeling sense, Seeing is loving because Seeing is totally dying for the other and really being annihilated for the other and it is not in the realm of feeling or thinking. It is more fundamental. It does not feel as one would expect love to feel, but I think it is, shall I say, a specially deep kind of loving. So deep the feeling is left floating. It goes beneath the feeling to the fact. It is not a kind of embryo loving or inferior loving, it is a culmination of loving. I think that if we look after the Seeing we will find ourselves able to leave the feelings to take care of themselves. Feelings will come and feelings will go as feelings always do. They will perhaps show some warming up, some improvement, perhaps not very much. But I think the great thing is to establish the foundation and base of love. Let the superstructure build itself, and demolish itself as it will.

Richard: Does Seeing give you peace?

Douglas: No, I don't think it does. I think it shows that I am peace. It doesn't give it to me or take it from me, it acquaints me with the region which is peace. So it doesn't give it, it points to its existence really. It points to that in me which is peace itself.

Richard: Does it make you feel at home in the universe?

Douglas: Again, if I might put it the other way, it makes the universe at home in me. To be at home in the universe suggests that there is a universe and there is me. A person, a thing, in a house, and the universe is my house, and I feel at home there. In a certain sense I suppose it could be looked at thus. But I would prefer to say that I am not at home in the universe until the universe is at home in me.

Richard: Is it important to have friends to share Seeing with?

Douglas: Yes, but I don't think it's essential. I think that obviously one can get along without such friends, and I had to for years. But it was a handicap and it made everything ten times more difficult. I think that one doesn't really know what friends and communication can be like until one shares Seeing with friends. Not only the joy of it but also the sharpening and deepening and widening of one's awareness. It is in every way helpful.

HOMEWORK

- When you next have a haircut, notice the scissors disappearing into and reappearing out of the void.
- When you go to the dentist, relax into being spacious (and toothless!).
- When talking on the phone, see how the phone disappears into nothingness. Two voices in one silence.
- When eating and drinking, notice the food and liquids disappearing into this bottomless hole that you are – an emptiness that becomes filled with taste!
- When you are with a friend, consciously be empty for him or her.

CHAPTER SEVEN

SEEING IS FOR EVERYONE

I hope the Course Comments show that Seeing is not just for a small group of people but is for anyone willing to look. It is, after all, the one thing – the one no-thing – which we all have in common. Everyone has access to this Consciousness, and everyone's response to it is equally valid. Of course our responses to this Consciousness, and the ways in which it affects us are different, but the Consciousness itself remains ever the same and always available.

Having friends who see who they really are is inspiring – seeing others living from the Source reminds us how valuable it is and encourages us to live from the Source too. If we don't have friends who see who they really are, then we can contact others through the Headless Way website, or make Seeing friends ourselves by sharing Seeing. It isn't *necessary* to know other seers, but sharing Seeing with others is encouraging, inspiring and fun.

If you meet up with other seers, why not do the No-Head Circle experiment together. One person could read out the text.

—EXPERIMENT 12—

The No-Head Circle

Stand in a circle with others – say between 3 and 10 people.

Put your arms round each other so that you are close and look down.

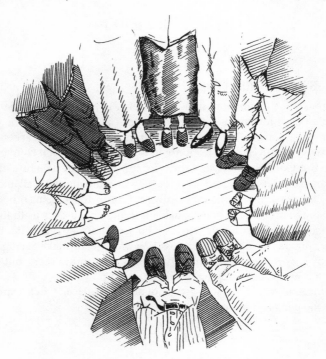

You see a circle of bodies. Each body in the circle is distinct. Down there you are separate from the others.

Notice that your body disappears above your chest into clear, boundless space, into your single Eye, into who you really are.

Notice that the other bodies also disappear above their chests, into the same clear space at the top of the circle that your body disappears into.

At the top of the circle you don't see several single Eyes – only one. There are no dividing lines in this space. When you put your no-heads together there's only one no-head. Everyone disappears into, and emerges out of, this one Consciousness. This Consciousness has no one's name on it. Everyone is in it. It belongs to all.

The thoughts and feelings of the others in the circle are hidden from you, but the one Self that belongs to everyone isn't hidden – it is visible at the top of the circle. When you see who *you* really are, you see who *everyone* really is.

Yet your awareness of this one Consciousness doesn't mean you ignore the differences down there in the circle – your single Eye has room for every point of view.

The no-head circle is like a round temple - the bodies are the circular wall. But as you can see this temple is ruined - there's no roof. This temple is wide-open to the clear, boundless sky. You are this infinite sky – the sky of being.

Who are you? You are the One that is Many.

SUPERHUMAN BEING

As we've seen, Douglas Harding (in his *Toolkit For Testing The Incredible Hypothesis*) indicates *what* to look for when we are looking for our true Self, *where* to look, and *how* to look. He also indicates *Who* to look for: 'a truly superhuman Being, with powers to match, and fully Self-aware.'

What powers are these? If you truly are the One in all beings, the Source from which the universe flows, what powers accompany your divine status? They are more obvious than you might think. Here is a fantasy that explores some of these powers, contrasting the powers of one's true Self with the lack of powers of one's human self.

The Powers of One's True Self

I am sitting on a beach with a friend. The sun is setting over the sea and the first star is peering down from the darkening sky. My gaze travels from that distant star down to the sun, further down to the sea, the shoreline and the sand, down to my feet and legs and torso. Further down, below my chest, I fade out. Stepping over this magical frontier into nothingness, I become everything. But when my friend looks down from the star, down and down and down, she doesn't vanish over any magical line. Only I have the power to disappear and become everything.

I close my eyes. (What eyes?) Sun, sea and sand disappear. I open my Eye – the scene springs back into view. But when my friend closes her eyes, nothing changes. Only the One has the power to destroy and create.

I put my hands over my ears (what ears?) and the roar of the waves fades away. That noisy seagull flying overhead is struck dumb. I remove my hands and the sounds surge back. My friend does the same but the seagull keeps squawking, the waves roar regardless. This One alone has the power to silence the world.

I look into the sky and the star catches my attention. It is light years away. Raising my hand I balance it on the tip of my finger. Both star and finger are here within me, no distance away. But there's nothing my friend can do to dissolve the distance between herself and that star, or between herself and anything. I look around. Wherever I look I am. Being no-thing, all things are within me. Only I am everywhere.

With the light of day fading we make our way to the house above the beach. Whereas my friend walks, I don't. I remain still whilst the world moves through me. This One alone sets the world in motion.

The house approaches. Measuring the doorway between my thumb and finger, I realize that if it stays so small, my body won't pass through it. But as I approach (as it approaches me) the doorway grows bigger, finally exploding to infinity – the perfect size for me. The next morning as I leave the house, I glance back and see the doorway shrinking. Only I have the power to make things grow and shrink - my friend has no such power. She must shrink to enter the house.

What Good Are These Powers?

'But what good are these powers? What's the point of making things disappear, shrink, grow, move, go silent…? It's a private experience of no practical value.'

It's true that I cannot show my powers to others or do anything with them. However, they are real to me. And they are significant because they are yet another demonstration to me of my divine identity.

I am like a king, in disguise as an ordinary citizen. My kingdom is the world. I am aware of my divine identity, yet it is my secret, for in my kingdom I appear as an ordinary citizen with no special powers. My real identity (with all my divine powers), though obvious to me, is hidden from others.

However, I have friends in my kingdom who are also aware of their divine identity. (A growing number of friends.) How delightful it is, sharing our experience of being the All-Powerful One in disguise – the One who appears as each and every one of us. Together we celebrate who we really are – the Hidden One, the Secret Magician, the Creator and Destroyer, the Unmoved Mover, the Universe-Traveller…

––––––––––––––

In his *Toolkit for Testing the Incredible Hypothesis,* Douglas Harding illustrates 5 powers: annihilating and re-creating the world; vanishing and re-appearing; astral travelling; making things grow and shrink; and moving things around. (In the above paragraphs we explored these powers.) He then explores the subject further, distinguishing between the 1st person (who we really are) and the 3rd person (our appearance):

Knowing All Things, Willing All Things, Having All Things, Being All Things

[The 1st person has observed how the 3rd person] lacks all the 5 powers; and common sense confirms that no mere man could begin to exercise the least of them.

So when *you* find yourself exercising them all – so naturally and effortlessly that you had (anyhow since early childhood) overlooked them altogether – the you in question is evidently far from being merely human.

Who, nearer than your feet and hands and breathing, could be so gifted?

Objection

These five Powers imply a superhuman being, no doubt, but hardly God. For, astounding though my Powers are, they leave much to be desired. Many things remain that are beyond (1) my knowledge, (2) my control, (3) my possession, (4) my self. For instance, I don't know what's on the next page, I can't make the letters on this page turn blue, I don't own that person's watch, and I'm not that other person, only myself. If God were here and I were Him, surely I would know all things, will all things, have all things, be all things?

Let us explore these 4 remaining, truly divine Powers.

Knowing All Things

With the help of your approaching (onion-peeling) observer, you found that you are *for others* a huge set of things – things astronomical, geographical, human, biological, chemical, physical (depending on the observer's distance from you) while remaining *for yourself* the No-thing at their centre, the Reality of which all those things are regional appearances.

Taking seriously your insight into the intrinsic Nature of objects of so many levels and kinds (all the way from a galaxy to atoms) what knowledge do you lack about things-in-themselves?

Or put it like this: in the world there's one thing of which you have true inside information – because you *are* that thing. Having every reason (as we've seen) to take this thing (or huge set of things) as a fair sample of the rest, you have complete inside information about them too.

As for knowledge, not of the one Reality but of its endless appearances, observe whether enough information isn't available at this moment (and at later moments when they come) for practical purposes, and whether much more coming in wouldn't confuse every issue. Wouldn't information about irrelevant appearances (such as what's overleaf) prove a particularly inhibiting kind of ignorance, and all-fussing rather than all-knowing?

Willing All Things

While seeing into your Voidness, seeing that you are Him now, notice whether you submit to, concur in, authorise, actually *will* whatever is. If you now have no separate will from His, aren't you (for the moment, anyhow) being Who you truly are?

Having All Things

Look carefully at your friend now. Having no face of your own, aren't you *obliged* to accept delivery of hers, so that it is much less hers than yours, and is yours most intimately? Isn't the same true of whatever you can see around the room, and hear, and feel, and think of? How could you have nothing of your own without having all it holds? With what could you refuse whatever presents itself – makes a present of itself – to you?

Take in the view from the window now – sky, clouds, hills, trees, houses – or at least take in the room and its furniture. How could all this be more yours, more given to and held by you, than it is at this moment? Aren't other moments just the same?

Look again at your friend. Could the one you see there begin to possess, really to hold, even one thing – her jacket, for instance, or watch – let alone all things? Can one who has a surface ever be well off?

Being All Things

Sit back comfortably, relax, be quite still, shut your eyes, and listen to your friend [reading the following questions]; answer her questions aloud only if you feel like it. (Then, read out the questions to her.)

On present evidence, what are you like now?

How many legs, arms, heads, bodies – if any – can you detect?

How big are you?

Can you truly say 'I am this, or that?'

Can you not nevertheless say 'I AM'?

Is your sense of BEING any less strong now than when you see or think of yourself as something or other? Is it, perhaps, much stronger now?

Is it dependent on any of your senses?

Has this I-AM-ness any features which could link it with your human aspect or anything else at all; or that could separate it from I-AM-ness however or wherever or whenever enjoyed?

Being thus at your own Centre, aren't you also at the Centre of all beings, of all BEING, and much nearer to them than their own hands and feet?

And much nearer to *me* than these hands and feet of mine?

Only have no mind of any kind, and this is known as undefiled knowledge.

HUANG-PO

~~~~~~~~~~~

If I knew myself as intimately as I ought, I should have perfect knowledge of all creatures.

MEISTER ECKHART

~~~~~~~~~~~

When the Self is seen, heard, thought of, known, everything is known.

BRIHADARANYAKA UPANISHAD

~~~~~~~~~~~

That thou mayest have pleasure in everything, seek pleasure in nothing. That thou mayest know everything, seek to know nothing. That thou mayest possess all things, seek to possess nothing.

ST JOHN OF THE CROSS

~~~~~~~~~~~

The understanding, the memory and the will are in a fearful void, in nothingness. Love this immense void. Love this nothingness since the infinitude of God is in it.

DE CAUSSADE

~~~~~~~~~~~

Others gain authority over you if you possess a will distinct from God's will.
RABBI NAHMAN OF BRATZLAV

~~~~~~~~~~~

With the removal of the 'I' illusion, the world with all its multiplicities will disappear, and if there is anything left which can act, this one will act with utmost freedom, with fearlessness, like the Dharma-king himself, indeed as the One.
D. T. SUZUKI

~~~~~~~~~~~

True wisdom is learning to wish that each thing should come to pass as it does.
EPICTETUS

~~~~~~~~~~~

He who clearly sees that, while treating things as things, he is no thing himself – how could he be content only to govern the hundred clans of the world...? He is the Sole Possessor.
CHUANG-TZU

~~~~~~~~~~~

Zen masters are totally identified with Nature.
D. T. SUZUKI

~~~~~~~~~~~

The word SUM, I AM, can be spoken by no creature, but by God only.
MEISTER ECKHART

~~~~~~~~~~~

The only being that is, is the Tao-man who, depending on nothing, is at this moment listening to my talk on the Dharma.
LIN-CHI

COURSE COMMENTS

I was raised in a farming community in vast open areas, surrounded by mountains. To go to school we travelled for an hour on a bus over hills and across valleys and plains. Something that I always had fun doing was imagining that it was the hills, and the trees, and the cows and sheep moving, and not me. And, finally, like in some movie that rolls on by, the town where our school was rolled into view, and then the general store, and post office, and finally it stopped passing us when the school reached the bus. Then the bus was moving and I found myself on the pavement outside... that was usually when it stopped but it was still fun :-) Spinning around in circles too was a favorite past-time of my friend and I so I understood what you meant when you said we stay still (and had fun doing it once again).

Donna

One thing which comes to mind and amuses me is my experience of travelling overseas. I'm from Australia, but now live in the USA. When I was flying in this huge jet over the Pacific Ocean I was lucky enough to have the window seat and watched as we left the tarmac at Sydney, flying off into no-thing. But once the plane had levelled out and was above cloudline it was like nothing moved. The plane didn't move, the clouds didn't move, it was just like sitting still. Indeed, had there not been a sign which stated how far we were from Los Angeles and how long it would be until we arrived I'd have probably gone insane because this feeling of utter stillness and not 'progressing' was driving me crazy. But when I wasn't wondering what on earth I was doing on a plane over the Pacific Ocean, I was watching this stillness, and meditating on the calm feeling the clouds radiated to me, and I felt ONE with them, like I could have just floated away with them. It was a very intense, profound feeling for me, especially when the clouds changed colour with the sun setting.

When you described the feeling of 'stress there, calm here', I was instantly reminded of how I felt when I was sitting in the plane watching the clouds and going no-where. :-) I can now, when I'm feeling stressed or worried, focus on my nothingness and feel one with everything around me, knowing that I stay still while these things move around me, but I am in touch with it all just the same. And the sense of calm washes over me; it's great.

I'm enjoying the class immensely and find it's a great review of headlessness. I first came across the headless website in March but wasn't ready for the material at that time. Then about 2 months ago I read all the material on the site and tried the experiments. What a revelation! I've been a seeker for almost 20 years and have had my share of insights but I couldn't believe how simple the Truth is or how easy to perceive it. I didn't realize that my True Nature was so near to me!

I've been a student of Advaita Vedanta for the last 10 years and have actually experienced headlessness before but couldn't figure out how to sustain the insight. The experiments offer a wonderfully simple way to do so and are fun too! I've been able to return to the original perception at any time for the last 2 months. The truth of who we are is so simple. Seeing really is knowing! Thank you and Douglas so much.

Today I was riding home in my car and I experienced being stationary while the world moved through me. Awesome!

Debbie

Sea Shell

What secret lies
in the heart of a sea-shell
you cannot tell.

But if one day
a shell on a rock should crack
and break its back

your gaze may fall
to find in its secret heart
nothing at all.

Then turning round
to the sea you may wonder
that the waves' sound

can come from an empty heart.

COLIN OLIVER

HOMEWORK

Exercise your powers:
- Destroy and re-create the world effortlessly.
- Set things in motion.
- Make things grow and shrink.
- Enjoy owning all things, being all things, willing all things...
- Share the Seeing with a friend, or two.

CHAPTER EIGHT

—EXPERIMENT 13—

The Unclassifiable

Imagine yourself in a room with about twenty people, sitting in a circle – or preferably do this, with someone taking my role – the role of leader. (You can play this game with smaller numbers.) I have a bag of small coloured stickers. Having asked everyone to close their eyes, I go round placing a sticker on everyone's forehead – yours included. You feel a sticker being attached but don't know what colour it is. When I've finished I ask you to open your eyes. (I close my own eyes whilst someone places a sticker on my forehead.)

There are three rules to the game: no talking, no looking in a mirror or other reflecting surface; and no touching any of the stickers.

I explain that the stickers come in four different colours. (There is not necessarily the same number of stickers for each colour.) Each corner of the room has a coloured sticker assigned to it, so there's a blue corner, red corner, etc.

Now I ask everyone to stand up and go to the corner designated for their colour. You have only a few seconds to do this.

You can see everyone else's sticker but you can't see your own. Can you work out which colour you are and go to the right corner, without breaking the three rules?

What are your reactions as you try and work out which colour you are? How do you feel if you can't solve the problem? How do you feel if you do get to the right corner? How did you do it? Can you be one hundred per cent sure that you are in the right corner?

There's a way of doing this and lessons to be drawn from the experience, but I'm not going to tell you how to do it. Try it for yourself. Gather a few friends together and do the experiment. Sit down afterwards and explore it's connection with headlessness.

A SUMMER'S DAY

I'm lying down in a meadow in long grass on a warm summer's day. A friend lies beside me, but I'm looking upwards so I don't see her. All I see is the blue sky in my wide single Eye, and stalks of grass rising out of the nothingness that I am. Clouds drift across the sky, from time to time a bird sings.

I raise my arm – an arm grows magically out of this transparent Ground, shooting up like one of those stalks of grass. I drop my arm and it's swallowed back down into the nothingness.

I remark on this to my friend whom I cannot see at the moment. A voice –

my voice – emerges from the silence. My friend replies – in this same silence. Our two voices dance in this one awareness as we talk - amazed, at our two voices dancing in this one silence.

Then the bird sings again, its silvery disembodied voice intermingling with our disembodied voices.

My friend continues talking, the bird sings on, but I fall silent. I am thinking about all of this. Who is thinking? My thoughts are as disembodied as my friend's voice and the bird's singing. They spring up I don't know how – from where? Then they are gone – where?

I hear my friend's voice again – she is pointing out a swallow, flying so high that I hadn't seen it till she drew my attention there. How beautiful this bird is, alone in the sky, so skilled in flight. Yet for itself it isn't a small bird – it's room for the vast sky and this swathe of English countryside below.

I love swallows. Seeing this one, my heart leaps with joy. My delight appears for a few moments in the clear sky of my being like that swallow in the sky, and then is gone. No one owns the swallow and no one owns my delight. I may call this delight mine, but in fact there is no me here to contain or hold it. Delight, and all my feelings and thoughts – all flow from nothingness into the world, just as my voice issues from the silence that I am.

I close my eyes. Still I have no boundaries. Sensations appear in the edgeless space of being. I name this sensation my leg, that one my back resting on the grass, another one my head, but there's no shape or colour or solidity evident at this moment. How big am I? Are these sensations inside me whilst the birdsong is outside me? I find no dividing line between myself and the world.

Images arise, but from where? They dissolve again, effortlessly. I feel the sun warm on my face. My face? The sun? With my eyes closed these are memories, images attached to that delicious feeling of warmth. The images themselves are unsupported, floating for a moment in awareness.

Unsupported? Suddenly I wonder if there is anything at all underneath me, around me. I experience a moment of panic as I feel vast space with nothing to hold onto.

Then I realise I am safe. Things come and go, feelings come and go, but the Awareness that all things arise from and fall back into remains steady, indestructible, reliable. Anything I try to hold onto will in the end crumble away, but this full nothingness, this I Am-ness, will never crumble, will never let me down. This is what I am, forever. Suddenly I realise I have been holding my breath. I relax and breathe again.

It's time to go. I open my eyes and the swallow has gone. I turn my head and find my friend's face, here in my emptiness.

How do you know but every bird that cuts the airy way, is an immense world
of delight, closed by your senses five?

WILLIAM BLAKE

~~~~~~~~

Seest thou the little wingéd fly, smaller than a grain of sand?
It has a heart like thee, a brain open to heaven and hell,
With inside wondrous and expansive; its gates are not closed;
I hope thine are not.

WILLIAM BLAKE

~~~~~~~~

When you have truly renounced the mind, you will see the whole universe in
yourself.

VASISHTHA

~~~~~~~~

Bodhisattvas are able to expand their bodies to the ends of the universe.

GANDAVYUHA SUTRA

~~~~~~~~

A sudden perception that Subject and object are one will lead you to a deeply
mysterious wordless understanding – you will waken to the truth of Zen.

HUANG-PO

~~~~~~~~

Let subject and object be so oned that the wind cannot pass between them.

WU-MEN

~~~~~~~~

I touch the sky with my finger,
Distance is nothing but a fantasy.

WILLIAM BLAKE

~~~~~~~~

Alone, without form or face,
Foothold or prop, one goes on
To love That, beyond all creatures,
Which may be won by happy chance.

ST JOHN OF THE CROSS

~~~~~~~~

COURSE COMMENT

After three lessons, I find the information very useful for opening my awareness, and sharing it with others... some hands-on stuff I can really use!! I can't
wait to continue with this course. Again, thank you for doing this for us.

Boundless

Like the wind searching,
lifting feathers round
the sparrow's neck,
lifting leaves in a wave
across the bean field,
I find no place
where I can say,
here my being ends.

COLIN OLIVER

ONGOING SEEING

Whenever you want to see who you really are, you can. It doesn't matter where
you are or what you're doing. Right now, as you read these words, you can see
that you are room for them, room for the whole process of reading.

Noticing you are capacity for the world doesn't get easier with time, simply
because this awareness is completely easy from the first moment you See, and
stays that way. How could your single Eye become more open, more obvious,
more accessible? However, what does change is how Seeing affects you. The
more you See, the deeper it goes.

How can we get into the habit of seeing who we really are? How do we make
sure we remember to look?

The main thing is *wanting* to remember. If you want to remember, you will.
The Seeing will spontaneously appear from the emptiness, so to speak. Suddenly you become aware you are Seeing, without having thought about it the
moment before.

But what if it doesn't happen spontaneously?

See now that you are capacity for these words...

Why are you suddenly Seeing now? Because these words about Seeing are
reminding you to See. Choosing to read this book means you have chosen to
do something that reminds you to See. If you have an important meeting to go
to but you don't trust yourself to remember, you put things in place that will
remind you. You might set an alarm, ask a friend to call you, or leave a note for
yourself. It's the same with Seeing. Do things that remind you. For example,

point at your no-face and look. Now you are aware of being capacity for your finger. Stand up, point at your emptiness and turn round. Now you are noticing you are the still centre of the turning world. Explore the edge of your single Eye with your hands. You are now seeing how wide you are – wider than the world! Sit quietly with your eyes closed and be the limitless space in which all arises. You are now conscious that thoughts, feelings, sounds and sensations are coming and going in your boundless emptiness, arising freshly from this mystery that you are. Look in a mirror for a minute and observe *where* your face is. You are now aware you are not what you look like. Arrange with a friend to do the face to no-face experiment together. Sitting opposite your friend, you are consciously being your friend. As you can see, you can use the experiments to remind you to See. They guide your attention immediately to who you really are.

You can extend the experiments into everyday life. When you are washing the dishes, rest your attention in the space from which your arms reach down into the sink. You are capacity for warm water, for your hands and cups and plates, for the sound of the tap running and the feel of your feet on the floor.

When you are driving, be aware that you go nowhere whilst your destination comes to you. Or if you are caught in traffic, relax into not being caught in traffic – it is caught in you. Be aware of the sound of the engine, the feel of the steering wheel, the other cars on the road, your thoughts and body sensations, all happening in who you really are. Perhaps you feel frustrated, but you notice you are the silent, perfectly relaxed space in which your frustration occurs. When you are at a checkout in a supermarket, notice you are capacity for the person serving you. Or meet for coffee with a friend and consciously be capacity for your friend and the conversation - face to no-face. If your friend is also Seeing, share your experience together. Two voices celebrating one Silence! Or when you find yourself in a tense situation with someone, be capacity for all that is happening, including the stress. Every situation is an opportunity to see who you really are.

Nevertheless, it's normal to forget and remember your true Self. It's a natural rhythm. I used to think that if I had forgotten to See, then I was doing something wrong, but I've changed my mind. Forgetting comes from the One, just like remembering does, and plays an important part. If I never forgot the One, I would never experience the joy of remembering it.

Nor does overlooking your true Self necessarily mean you don't value it. If you don't think of someone you love every minute of the day, does this mean you don't love them enough? Of course not. They are still present in your heart. It's the same with the One – sometimes it's in the foreground of your awareness, sometimes in the background. If it's in the background, you can bring it forwards whenever you wish, instantly.

Having said which, I do want to remember, I do want to see this treasure and enjoy this blessing as often as I can: now, and now, and now…

COURSE COMMENT

It seems to me that *The Unclassifiable* game is the game we have been playing all our lives. We've all been searching around with different coloured 'faces' looking for our place to belong. It's the 3rd- person game. We can only find our place by the acceptance of others if the colour is right.

Seen from the 1st person, I don't have a face to stick a sticker on, only others need to stick a sticker on their view of my face if they are playing the game. There is no area to go to: all is within me. The game is just the presumed 3rd person searching for what it thinks it needs. From now on it is just the 1st person. No search, no needs, no person, just 'is'. Thank you for opening the door.

Closer is He than breathing, and nearer than hands and feet.
ALFRED, LORD TENNYSON

~~~~~~~~

The strange fact is that when a door opens and a light shines from an unknown source into the dark chamber of consciousness, all time and space limitations melt away, and we make a 'Simhanada' (lion-roar): 'Before Abraham was, I am,' or 'I alone am the Honoured One above and below the heavens.'
D. T. SUZUKI

~~~~~~~~

What I call perfection of vision is not seeing others but oneself.
CHUANG-TZU

~~~~~~~~

If you want peace of mind and true unity of purpose, you must put all things behind you and look on yourself.
THOMAS À KEMPIS

~~~~~~~~

I will see if I have no meaning, while the houses and ships have meaning.
WALT WHITMAN

~~~~~~~~

Forgetfulness of the Self is the source of all misery.
RAMANA MAHARSHI

SEX AND SEEING

What are the implications of seeing who you really are in the intimate area of sexual relationships? The following article discusses this important subject.

Sex and Facelessness

Douglas Harding, from *The Toolkit for Testing the Incredible Hypothesis*

When sexual partners see into their True Nature and are consciously faceless together, their loving can come to them as a revelation, an opening out upon new and unsuspected dimensions of existence. At the same time it remains as human (and certainly as physical) as ever - except that it is remarkably steady and unanxious and free from the usual self-concern and grasping. More surprising, perhaps, is the discovery that it can promote the seeing of both partners.

Surely the reason is that this love, though too rare, is in fact only natural. *All* true lovers are, however unconsciously, face to no-face and, conversely, *all* the consciously faceless are, at least in the profoundest sense, true lovers. This is how our love-life is lived when we stop pretending: really we are built this way and have no choice - *even more built for loving above the belt than below.* Here at the top which is always topless, each always fits the other like a skintight glove, each is a perfect receptacle ready for and needing to be filled out with the other, absolutely female to the other's maleness, unreservedly given and self-abandoned and overcome and penetrated. Here is an ideally asymmetrical union, a unique fusion, not of body with body (which is impossible, since each body fills only its own volume) nor of spirit with spirit (which is superfluous if not absurd, since spirit is indivisible) but of body with spirit, so that each is the other. Here indeed, in the upper region of love's embrace, form is Void and Void is form, and lovers achieve their otherwise unattainable goal: they vanish in favour of, they actually become, each other. No wonder the face - provided there's only one present - and the eyes in particular - provided there are only two - can for such lovers be the best aphrodisiac of all! *Vive la différence* - the absolute difference between the 1st person as the faceless lover and the 2nd person as the loved face - especially since it gives birth to the whole world! Whereas living together face-to-face (surely living in sin, the sin of imagined symmetry, divorcing body and spirit) means mutual impenetrability - leading to rejection, fear of union, life at loggerheads, lovelessness, sterility - so living together face to no-face (in the true union of body and spirit) means their cure. Whether or not it includes sex, the face to no-face relationship means the enjoyment of that ultimate intimacy which knows no hang-ups or hang-overs and is incapable of perversion or surfeit or disillusion; and if up here at eye-level occurs such a marvellous interpenetration that each wholly replaces the other, such penetration as may be occurring lower down could hardly fail to be enriched. If the higher level is lacking, what hope for the lower? Can any lover know what love is who prudishly refuses entry to the loved one's face (as if it were possible!) by always thrusting his or her own in the way? Can any lover *fail* to know what love is who submits to this invasion so delightedly, when to look at is to die for the loved one?

In short, so far from ruling out physical love, Self-realisation can usefully employ it; and, so far from ruling out Self-realisation, physical love positively demands it. To neglect our hypothesis is to thwart and curtail our earthly human love as well as the diviner sort, by separating them. Ultimately sex doesn't come into its own till it is revealed as an aspect of the One's own joy in discovering and reuniting with Itself, disguised as the not-self or other - as one very special other.

For, however faceless it may be, a diffused love - a general embracing of all beings - is by itself rather facile and vague and diluted, and likely to lack in depth what it gains in breadth. Fortunate is the one who also enjoys a faceless *concentrated* love - a singular adoration for one person, normally but by no means necessarily expressed in sexual union - a unique interfusion in which the loved one nevertheless stands for everyone, so that (in a way hard to describe) each is specially loved in and through that special loved one. Can anybody who has thrilled to this particular love doubt that it is an essential clue to what the world is all about?

Of course the sexual implementing of this particular love is necessarily restricted in practice and, more often than not, ruled out altogether. But such limitations, however painful they may sometimes prove, are eventually acceptable by the faceless who (as such) enjoy complete union in any case. Intercourse is a poignant but optional or dispensable extra for them, because there is always to hand this supreme Interfusion, this Identity which, in the last resort, lacks nothing.

Sex and Self-Awareness

At the physical level, no such perfection is to be expected. A couple who, besides seeing - intermittently - how one they are in the One, have come to express this union sexually, aren't necessarily and immediately without sexual difficulties. But they should know what to do about them. 'Whatever the problem, its solution is never to lose sight of the Self *in any circumstances.*' What, not even in bed? Not even when the problem is a sexual one? Not even in orgasm? Specially not then! What kind of Resource is it, that can cope with ordinary difficulties but not with ones like this? If our hypothesis is valid, if Self-seeing works, it works here too; and if it doesn't it is indeed dubious. And in fact the evidence so far is that it works no less well in this delicate and important field than in any other.

Take, for instance, a common trouble - self-consciousness interfering with sexual performance or responsiveness. This is, after all, only a particular case of morbid self-consciousness in general, and its treatment is the same. Of course one tries to forget oneself, to lose oneself in one's partner, but the attempt is doomed from the start - the harder one tries the more self-occupied one gets. The only real cure isn't less self-consciousness but more - more of that true Self-consciousness which is seeing one's Absence, instead of that self-consciousness which is trying to overlook one's presence. (And, remember, this Absence can never be partially or dimly seen; nor should the seeing of It be too hard to maintain here, since It is the indispensable Canvas on which that loved face is painted.)

The wonderfully strange and happy fact is that *this Self-seeing (which is perfect anyway) IS self-forgetting*: with the result that (for example) the once painfully-self-occupied public speaker, now wholly occupied with the audience, talks fluently and spontaneously and unanxiously; and the once painfully-self-occupied lover, now wholly occupied with the beloved, loves similarly well. In falsely self-conscious loving, which begins by being inefficient and ends by being impossible, each is using the other for personal satisfaction; each is attempting to enjoy his or her own body instead of the other's - so the enjoyment dwindles. In truly Self-conscious loving, on the contrary, each is the disembodied enjoyer of the other's body; each consciously makes way for and is occupied by the other, feels the other, knows (in the biblical sense) the other - and the by-product or bonus is that physical enjoyment flourishes, perhaps as never before.

The pattern (the form-is-Void pattern) is displayed at all levels. Starting at the top, where it manifests visually as face to no-face, it manifests non-visually lower down as body to no-body and genitals to no-genitals. For provided one attends to what's actually given, the known abolishes the knower and the object ousts the organ that senses it: so that one smells a rose and not a nose, hears drums and not eardrums, touches this page and not fingertips. Genuine love-making is equally simple, equally non-dual and self-effacing, when the lover ceases playing Peeping Tom at his own bedroom keyhole, and becomes an Absentee in respect of all his senses. Imagined symmetry is just as damaging - because as fictitious - below the belt as above. But when it is corrected up there (how easy to disappear for that face!) it is at least well on the way to being corrected below, where symmetry may not be so easy.

The trouble - this illusion of symmetry - getting off to a slow start in early childhood and rapidly coming to a head in early youth, is the all-too-human knack of going out from oneself and there turning in upon oneself, so as to treat oneself as a mere object, a thing to handle among things to handle, a 2nd or 3rd person, a body, a face, genitals - with all the guilt and anxiety this manoeuvre is apt to entail. (Unlike more primitive animals, and notably unlike the neckless and limbless fish, the shape and flexibility of man's body invite him thus to work on himself and build himself up, to body himself forth from his native Emptiness.) The development of this self-thinging-knack up to and into adult life takes the form of playing simultaneously two master-games - the Face Game and the Genitals Game (strictly, the My-face-here Game and the My-genitals-here Game), both of them starting as simple hand-games but going on to great subtlety and complexity. Both involve handling, caressing, manipulating, concentrating on, enjoying, loathing one's own body - in one case the upper part of it, in the other the lower. The first - working up a face *for oneself* - is a sort of public masturbation; the second - working up a sex-organ *for oneself* - is the private kind; but the endeavour, and even the means, are strikingly similar, and the tragic consequences are the same - inability to love, since *things* (faces, bodies, genitals) as such are loveless. Learned at the same time and inextricably linked throughout one's early years, it would be fitting and natural if these twin master-games could be unlearned together, if they could simultaneously yield to the same basic therapy - which is none other than our hypothesis itself put into practice. Here, un-thinged in consciously asymmetrical loving, one may lose (a double operation, how suitably celebrated!) 'all the shame of having a face' and all the shame of having genitals. The teenager does indeed have reason to be shamefaced: it *is* shameful to have and to be such things *here*. It makes bad sense, and consequently bad love.

Who after all, is here? Who is this Present-absent One, this No-thing, this 1st Person Singular, present tense? Haven't we decided that He is the one eyeless Seer, the one earless Hearer, the one tongueless Taster? He is also the one bodiless Lover! And just as the lover sees the beloved's face through a conceptual fog while he thinks he sees it with his eyes, and muffles the sound of her voice while he thinks he hears it with his ears, so he hardly begins to love her body while he thinks he loves it with his body. Only when he submits to being the One he really is - and she really is - does he know how to love that body, and know what sex is really about. In order to love it is necessary to be God, for God is love - and, not least, physical love. In order to be truly one with another it is necessary to be the One who is that other.

All the same, the practical testing and implementing of our hypothesis - in particular, seeing the Infinite Basis of loving - isn't going to perfect Its finite instruments overnight, or completely. To live is to be in difficulties. But our necessarily limited human nature will have its knots progressively untwisted till it becomes truly human and natural - and acceptable just as it happens to be, out there where it belongs. What sexual 'problems' remain will no longer appear problematical and distressing, now that they are viewed from their problem-free Centre and Origin. The homosexual, for instance, may still have to live with his deviation, but he can more cheerfully do so when, seeing that intrinsically he is the Source of all the varieties of sex, he finds in that Source the one essential 'Normality' which unites him absolutely with all creatures whatsoever, independent of the local and temporary accidents of sex and biological evolution. And so with every sexual difficulty - whether it is lack of a sexual outlet (on account of social prohibition or personal inhibition), or impotence or frigidity, or any sort of abnormality or malfunctioning - our hypothesis implies that seeing-Who-has-the-difficulty is the only radical treatment. Surely, if anything will work, this will. The evidence, which is only beginning to come in, is indeed encouraging. But each lover, or loving couple (again: the decisive tests are two-person), has to discover whether this seeing is as practical in bed as out of it.

Rewards

Douglas Harding, from *Look For Yourself*

I promise you that the rewards will be proportional to the seriousness and persistence of your Homecoming. But they will be unique to you, and I can't predict them in any detail. There are four things, however, that I can safely say:

1. The more you go for the real truth and the less for the rewards, the more rewards you will get.

2. You will tap new energies. This is because you are breaking the exhausting habit of eccentricity, and instead are tapping the Source of all energies within, at Centre.

3. You will find yourself approaching the unself-consciousness and spontaneity that you enjoyed as a child. With this difference: then you simply lived from your Home, now you do so with full awareness. But now, as then, you are Space for the people around you to occupy, and by no means one of them. The freedom, the relief, is awesome. Specially if, like me, you had suffered excruciatingly from shame-facedness.

4. In effect, you will perceive that you are built for loving. That's to say that... you are Empty for the loved one. You vanish in favour of – you give your life for – that one. The feeling follows the vision. Your heart opens, your love starts to flow naturally and freely.

Be patient. Don't demand that these or any other blessings will be apparent at once.

HOMEWORK

- Attend to Who you really are, anywhere, anytime...
- Do an experiment from time to time.
- Washing up, see who is washing up.
- When talking with a friend, hear your two voices in the one Silence.

PART II

Articles, Correspondence and Interviews

ARTICLES

The Bomb

Alain Bayod

I have certainly nothing very special to say about Seeing but I would not wish to miss the opportunity offered to me by Richard Lang to manifest my huge gratitude to Douglas.

I am French, 49 years old, and I have been practising yoga since my teens and studying advaita vedanta for the last twenty years. Of course, it has gradually made big changes in my life but I have felt for several years that I was at a dead-end, stuck in the rut of my ego. In spite of long and accurate psychological work on the unconscious I was in search of a key.

My meeting with Douglas and Catherine Harding was for me a sort of fairy tale. Though the book *On Having No Head* was on my shelves for ten years, it was impossible for me to read it. The picture on the cover looked very bizarre and the text quite obscure. Three years ago a friend of mine published a book on 'the new sages of the West'. The last chapter was on Douglas Harding and I was not really interested. I thought, of course very superficially, that the teaching of this Englishman was not at all traditional. Moreover it looks weird. And above all he never had a real-life guru. It was not for me.

But a few months just after that premature judgement another friend who already knew Douglas and enjoyed Seeing suggested that I invite Douglas and Catherine to Ardenne, the spiritual centre in the south-west of France where I have lived and worked since 1982.

I do not know why, but strangely I accepted immediately, although without enthusiasm. The workshop was fixed for the 1st of November. It was 1993. When I welcomed Douglas at Bordeaux station and therefore met him for the first time, a kind of alchemy occurred. He moved me in a very positive way and I thought: 'Although his teaching has no interest for me, it is really worthwhile to meet such a lovely octogenarian.'

About forty of my pupils were there and the workshop started. Instead of my reticence, I decided to play the game openly. But I did not expect any result, and I now realise that it was perhaps the best attitude with which to start the 'No-face game'. A vacant mind, no desires, no expectations. As the Zen man said, 'the beginner's mind'. At the end of the first day, after the pointing and the third-eye experiments, I had not yet got the point. But something was moving and I felt that I was on the verge of a great discovery. During dinner, with a smile, Douglas told me, 'Tomorrow I will put a bomb in Ardenne', and indeed it was so.

I think I shall never forget that morning. Of course, the bomb was the paper tube, the most powerful deconditioning device actually in existence. I entered the tube with a friend at the other end. How many faces in the tube? One, only one! What do you see on present evidence on your side of the tube? Good heavens, nothing at all but a clear empty space, nothing at all to deny the face there.

This space was totally naturally and simply one with my friend's face, and also one with thoughts and feelings. I was this free and aware space. No more confrontation of my ego with anything. The bomb had exploded. This first experiment took place eighteen months ago and I can simply say that it was a cataclysmic event.

Since that day my spiritual practice, my teaching, in short my whole life, has completely changed in a profound way. But that is another story.

To be at one with the world as I had tried unsuccessfully for years is simply to be nothing at all. To love is to disappear in favour of another person. It was really a very powerful and dangerous bomb. Nothing remains here to deny the world.

The Hill

David Lang

Recently I read a cartoon in which a woman is saying to a friend, 'Jo, I think I'm depressed because I'm getting closer and closer to 40.' To which Jo replies, 'Look on the bright side, Wendy. In a few years you'll be getting farther and farther away from 40.'

I know what Wendy is talking about, for over the last few years I've felt a growing resistance to getting older. Each year I have adjusted upward my idea of when middle age begins. I have become suspicious of the mirror. And I have begun to rationalize that I must have been born with a receded hairline. However, it's becoming clear that I'm losing the argument as well as my hair. My peers now look middle aged. Twenty-year-olds appear much younger than they used to. And I'm coming up against an indisputable point. Next year I will be 40. No-one can push the start of middle age beyond that. 'Wow', I exclaim, 'whoever believed it would really happen!' Yet there it is, no longer on the distant horizon but right in front of me: The Hill. And although Jack Benny managed to dig his heels in at 39 and for years avoided making the final step onto the summit of that dark mountain, I have no such magic. Next year I'll be standing there, and in a year or two I'll be over the hill and gathering speed on the fast slide down the other side.

Of course, my own resistance to growing old is characteristic of our culture. How often we try to distance age with surgery, regressive behaviour, or well-meaning compliments. For the idea of getting old evokes great fears: of being lonely, vulnerable, sick, or poor, to name a few. And what happens to us after we get old, if not before? Death lurks invisibly like a black hole ready to suck in and annihilate our bodies and minds and everything we have valued in our lives.

Forty: a one-way ticket making me say goodbye forever to the young person I used to be. It is a humbling leavetaking, for along with acknowledging my departed youth, I am having to let go of my adolescent fantasies. These are harder to release; a deeper self-image is at risk. But being near the top of The Hill gives me a long view back on my life. The patterns are clear. I can see who I have and have not been, and I do not see the person I fantasized I would be by now. I am being forced to face the fact that my dreams of making a splash in the world in one way or another were misguided and arose out of an emotional need for attention. The overwhelming probability is that I will come and go in this world with only a few friends and acquaintances ever knowing that I came and went. When they are dead, I will be gone completely. Already, the bold lines around my much-desired significance are fading. I merge into crowds, anonymous as the faces staring out of old photographs in museums. When I am dead, my only lasting footprints will be a few entries in institutional records. Some splash!

However, this depressing scenario is misleading, for if I avoid as far as possible the fearful reaction, the attempt to regroup, the renewal of ambition in the campaign to be someone in the world, and instead surrender to the fact that I am the original Nobody, then the dead-end of obscurity becomes the main road of self-acceptance. When I choose as my only goal the Void, I can accept more easily that as a person I am limited and weak; that I am special in a few ways but ordinary in a lot more ways; and that I will soon die and be forgotten. And strangely, I discover that there is relief in being able to admit, even embrace, all this. There is relief too in seeing my human identity sink back into the crowd and the photograph where it belongs instead of trying to get it up on a pedestal separate from other people. In saying goodbye to not just my youth but to my whole human life, I can allow it to go home to where it belongs. And no longer quite so blinded by the need to see myself as significant, I can at last look back on my life and get to know myself as I have been rather than as I wanted to be. And I can be kind to myself.

But there is even better news than this. In being prompted by the visions from The Hill to shift emphasis away from needing to stand out among people and toward surrendering more fully to the Void, I inherit many qualities that flow directly out of the Emptiness. And while they are not quite as central or reliable as the Emptiness, they make a remarkable difference to the quality and meaning of life. For example, less distracted by the need to be creative to impress people, I can take my creativity as the Void much more seriously. As a result, I begin to own unbelievable creativity: the effortless beauty of sparrows singing in the Silence, a freeway vibrating with trucks in the perfection of the Given, and the singular face of a stranger glanced at on a street. The mysterious stars, difficult times, innocent children, all flow directly and easily from this central Emptiness. These are the real splashes in life, waves of great power and spontaneity crashing on the long shore of the Void. Everywhere I look are the creative expressions of this Nobody who has no other to impress. Compared to this level of creativity, 'personal' creativity is marginal. And creativity is just one example of the riches of the Nobody. The perspective from The Hill also prompts me to own the immortality, the steadiness, the mysteriousness and the resourcefulness of the Void. Paradoxically, the more I listen to what age tells me, the more I hear the songs of eternity.

In a real sense, of course, no-one can own or control these riches. In fact, this is the beauty of the arrangement, for it is only as No-one, as Emptiness that is surrendered and seeks nothing and is prepared for the worst, that I can experience the deeper joys as they flit in and out of Being, weaving patterns with the many dark emotions I will never cease to experience. And only as No-one can I value these joys and riches. My person cannot profit from them, cannot find that longed-for splash by claiming them as badges of specialness. Such a claim would tarnish them and would send me headlong down the slippery and scary slope to isolation and death.

And so it turns out that, contrary to much of what our culture tells us about growing old, The Hill offers us an opportunity and a blessing. When seen for the gift it is, age can motivate us, as in part it motivated the Buddha, to surrender to the Ageless and find there the real fulfilment of our potential. Anything that can do that is worth looking into.

A Useful Tool & Much More

Nick Smith

I first experienced headlessness in early summer of '94 and it gave me direct access to lots of things that hitherto I had only lots of written evidence for and that seemed to make sense but was still remote and intangible.

The workshop had quite an impression on me and I carried the ideas away and worked on incorporating them into my life. The first I experienced after doing an exercise with a paper tube – just looking down it into someone's face filling the other end.

The coaching for the exercise was to focus more on our own end of the tube rather than staring at the other person. My end of the tube felt vast and I experienced a profound sense of being the front end, if you like, of something huge.

It really did feel like I had the backing of the universe and I had the sensation that I could even lean backwards and be supported physically.

For years I've read literature of all denominations and philosophies talking about oneness and our separateness only being an illusion, but nothing gave me tangible physical access to this in the way that my headless experience did.

I've also believed that I am more than just my physical appearance/my body and headlessness gave me a real experience of this in a way that words cannot adequately describe. I will however share three things I experienced, two on the workshop and one in a hotel some weeks later.

The first thing was just a comment from a fellow participant on a workshop when she announced that she was going to pour some water into the void and my perception of eating and drinking altered dramatically. To which someone added, 'Only God tastes, smells and hears'.

The second was during an exercise where instead of perceiving the world through the two eyes we see when looking in a mirror, we actually looked out as if through one eye and then we were only limited as to the width of our vision by the width of the room.

Someone mentioned at this stage that they knew a friend who 'wore the stars as a hat'. I had a good belly laugh to this but it also helped me shift to a new level of awareness that feels really simple yet incredibly profound.

The third experience I had was a few weeks later and is similar to the 'stars as a hat' example. I was in a hotel room on a business trip and whilst setting up for my morning meditation session I felt disturbed as my normal habit is to sit in the centre of the room – and the way the room was laid out meant this was not possible. It was here I started laughing to myself as I thought that once I was meditating with my eyes closed the fact I was not physically positioned in the centre of the room made no difference at all as I could free myself from any perceptual limitations.

I realise as I write that these experiences are quite difficult to convey but I hope they may whet your appetite if not satisfy it.

I'll finish by sharing two ways in which headlessness has a really practical application.

First, in my job quite often I have to speak in front of lots of people and I find that by trading faces with the audience I'm nowhere near as affected by the difficulties.

Secondly, by far the most valuable way in which I've learned to use headlessness is in being able to listen to people and really get myself out of the way (literally) so I can hear them without judging or assessing them – which I believe is the greatest service we can provide for our fellow man.

The Still Centre

Richard Lang

Whoever says that the Tathagata goes or comes, sits or lies down,
he does not understand the meaning of my teaching.

THE DIAMOND SUTRA

In his workshops the philosopher and spiritual teacher Douglas Harding invites people to do awareness exercises, or experiments as he calls them. Their purpose is to wake you up to who you really are. One of these experiments involves movement. You stand up and point at your face. What do you see? Of course you don't see your face. Your finger points at nothing – or No-thing (which is simultaneously full of everything). Then you start turning round on the spot. What moves? The scenery beyond your finger moves past, but your side of your finger nothing moves – for there is nothing here to move. Put another way, you stay still whilst the world moves. Simple? Naive? Childlike? Yes – all of these. And also true and profound.

Last Autumn I flew to New York. Before leaving London I thought about the journey ahead. Looking out of the still No-thingness of my true nature into my quiet living room, I was aware that soon I would be looking out into busy, lively New York – from this same No-thingness. The scene was about to change radically, yet I would go nowhere. I decided to see if this proposition was really true: 'Every so often during this trip I will check to see if I have actually gone anywhere.'

So when the taxi arrived at six in the morning and I was whisked off through the empty streets of London, I saw that it was not I that was moving but the houses and lampposts. Arriving at Heathrow I realised it was still true – I had gone nowhere. The airport had arrived in me. Then the plane and all its passengers appeared in me. And at last New York, and the friend I was staying with, sprung to life in my stillness.

My reason for visiting New York was to attend a dance therapy training – the first module of a series of three, all taking place in the States. This first ten-day course was on Broadway and I found my way there the next morning. An hour or so into the course and I was dancing in the midst of sixty people – some of whom I already knew from other dance workshops. In the middle of this sea of bodies I realised that still I had gone nowhere. These sixty floating, whirling, stamping, breathing bodies had arrived in me. They were dancing in my stillness, in my living room – the Living Room or Space of my true nature. I felt as though I were hosting a big party at home!

Whilst in New York I visited a friend in Brooklyn. Actually, I had previously only corresponded with Joel over the internet, but he had been to a workshop with Douglas Harding and valued this simple inseeing into one's clear – and still – true nature. So I felt we were already friends. I arrived at his apartment and sat down to dinner with him and his wife. I told them about my experiment – to see whether or not I moved whilst on my trip to New York. 'And although it is true for you that I have arrived at your dinner table from London, and am your guest in your home, my experience is that I have gone nowhere and you have arrived here in me. It is you that are guests in my home!'

This reminds me of a story I heard recently about Einstein – I have no idea whether or not it is true. One evening Einstein was out visiting friends. After dinner the conversation continued in their drawing room. It began to get late. Finally Einstein yawned, remarked that it was past his bedtime, and asked if his friends wouldn't mind now going home!

Being still whilst the world moves through you is the way things are. It is also relaxing and good for your health. Douglas Harding, now in his nineties, travels the world giving workshops. About ten years ago a friend of mine asked him, 'How come you don't seem to get tired, Douglas? You do so much travelling.' To which Douglas replied, 'Well, you see, I never go anywhere!'

Now, after my journey to New York, I am back home in my living room, still looking out of No-thingness. It is true – I haven't moved an inch. Yet many places have appeared and disappeared in me.

On Being Aware

Douglas Harding

Awareness is what life's all about. At least, it's what I'd like my life to be about. At the end of it I want to be able to say, truthfully, that I was aware – awake, attentive to what's going on, not dreaming or "out to lunch".

I don't mean aware all the time of course, but often, increasingly, to the best of my ability. Naturally I like having lovely feelings, enjoying peak experiences when they arrive, perhaps even taking off into mystical realms. But when they don't include experiencing *who* is in receipt of all such goodies, why then they're a sort of lapse into unawareness and (at best) pleasant vacations from the main business of my life – namely being really aware. Which means *self*-aware, and ultimately *Self*-aware.

Such were my first reflections on hearing of *Aware* [the name of the magazine that first printed this article, in 1981]. I was reminded of those talkative birds in Aldous Huxley's *Island*, who startled the forest-walker by squawking out *"Attention!"*, relentlessly. They had come under Buddhist influence. And indeed their message is central to that religion.

Mindfulness, or attention, or awareness lies at the heart of Buddhism. It's not only the path to enlightenment, but enlightenment itself – that "state" which could be described as total awareness.

Awareness of precisely what?

Obviously not of just any old thing. The object or content of awareness matters as much as its intensity or steadiness. What yellow-robed monk could be more mindful (less absent-minded) than the thrush that at this moment is hauling a worm out of my lawn? What holy man can become more one-pointed than he was as an infant, playing with a ball on the grass? The absorption of bird and baby in what's going on is just about total – while it lasts.

But neither is *enlightened*. True, it isn't, like most of us grown-ups practically all the time, deluded. On the other hand it certainly isn't self-aware – even to the limited extent that we're self-aware. (That bird overlooks its presence; the sage sees his absence – a very different way of life, as we shall presently observe for ourselves.) And certainly the infant and the bird aren't for imitating, even if we knew how.

But this is jumping ahead. Let's proceed step by step, and distinguish in more detail the three stages in the development of awareness – stages which apply equally to the evolution of humanity in general, and of the individual in particular. Simply for convenience I'll call them: (1) Primitive (infrahuman) Awareness, (2) Human (lack of) Awareness, and (3) Enlightened (suprahuman) Awareness.

Primitive (infrahuman) awareness

To the examples of the thrush with the worm and the baby with the ball, we could add the worm itself (before its fatal encounter with the thrush), patiently edging and nosing and fitting a fallen leaf into its hole. (How the dear thing does it with a body like that, is a miracle of dexterity – and attention. You or I would have a job, using all ten fingers!) And why not add the example of one of that gifted creature's nerve cells (all unknowingly involved in that same delicate task of leaf-work) as it minds its own cellular business of attending to each incoming neural message and passing it on to the right quarters?

In fact, I'd go much further, and suggest that the *inside* story of each of the worm's cells, and each of that cell's molecules, and so down to whatever the ultimate units or building blocks of the "physical" world might be, is nothing else than awareness. Awareness of its companions, of its world. How otherwise could its responses to them be so accurate, appropriate or consistent? Each particle "knows" its job to perfection and does it superbly: it takes in (note that expression) and adjusts minutely to the mass and position and motion of all the other particles, everywhere.

Now there's awareness for you! No electron, no atom, no molecule, no cell, no bird, no animal is ever "out to lunch", or found guilty of driving (or flying, or swimming, or creeping, or whatever its favoured mode of locomotion) without "due care and attention". But my message isn't addressed to that overwhelming majority of the universe's citizens – the careful and conscientious sort who don't need it – but to us cosmic delinquents and scatterbrains who need it badly. To the only absent-minded creatures in the known universe.

Human (lack of) awareness

Let's take a closer look at what's happened to us, of the second stage:

Suppose I'm a keen bird-watcher, and find myself fascinated by that thrush's goings-on. I set myself the task of counting how many worms it manages to get down per hour.

Intrigued and even horrified though I am, I find that, after very few minutes of attention to that guzzling, single-minded creature on the ground, I'm up and away. I'm off on some flight of the imagination – planning, perhaps, this article I'm writing which features the thrush, or about the tummy ache it's surely going to have if it carries on like this. Or wondering what it feels like being a worm, tugged at and stretched as if it were an elastic band, and then being carved up into wriggling bird-helpings.

Meantime, of course, the bird carries on unobserved. I leave even the garden behind, as I'm carried away into exalted reflections about dear old Mother

Nature – so "red in tooth and claw", and beak; and even more exalted reflections about the problem of pain in the universe. I end my morning's stint at "bird-watching" by wondering what *I've* got for lunch – vaguely hoping it isn't spaghetti!

Bare attention to the scene that's presented right now, stripped clean of memory, anticipation, judgement: let's face it, for us humans this is practically impossible. We see what we're looking for, what we're told to see, what language allows us to see, what we can make some use of – even when, ever so briefly, we're staring hard at the worm, the bird, the baby, the flower, or whatever, doing our best to see it as it is. What's more, I fear that the older and better informed we grow, the more scatterbrained (not to say scatty!) we become. The absent-minded professor is no mere story put around by rude students. Didn't Isaac Newton himself boil his watch, timing it with his egg?

There is a sense, of course, in which Newton was one of the most aware people of his time, of any time. He was a giant, taking in… but what didn't he take in? And no doubt we all become aware of more and more as we grow up. The field of attention and its topography widen wonderfully. But, offsetting this gain, our awareness becomes increasingly contaminated by verbal comment, by superimposed mental stuff which blurs and almost obliterates the scene. We see the world through a thickening fog. For some of us the visibility is reduced to the point when we are certified "mad". We come to live in a dream world of our own, altogether out of contact with "reality", and in need of institutional care. Buddhists tell us we're all somewhat crazy like this – until we are enlightened.

They go on to say that it is this failure to attend to what's so, which is our undoing, our basic trouble. "The way," says the Buddha, "to resolve trouble and disharmony, get beyond bodily and mental suffering, and tread the path that leads to Nirvana, is by practising mindfulness" – mindfulness of the body, of sensations, of mental states, of conceptions. Which indicates how practical is the subject under discussion. We all want to suffer less, to get our deepest anxieties cleared up. Awareness, they tell us, is the way.

What to do? One thing is certain from the start: we can't revert to infancy, and certainly not to the one-pointedness of non-humans. But we can go on to train ourselves in mindfulness, precisely as people train themselves in figure skating, or chess, or singing, step by step under the guidance of experts.

Theravada Buddhism consists, very largely, of this training in mindfulness. For example, the exercise of mindful walking – walking in very slow motion, when every little sensation of touch, tension, and muscular adjustment is carefully noted. (To the irreverent spectator, one appears to have reverted to the reptilian stage of our ancestral history; but who cares when the advertised rewards are so great?) Or mindful breathing, when perhaps for hours the trainee "watches" and counts his in-breathings and out-breathings. At first he quickly forgets what he's supposed to be doing and stops counting, but with long practice he improves. And so with all the chores of the day – mindful dressing and undressing, mindful eating and defecating, and so on, till every moment is rescued from unawareness.

Costing so much in time and effort, it's as well that the advertised benefits of such discipline are impressive. Here are five of them. FIRST, what's done attentively is done better. Notice your visitors helping by washing the dishes: the mindful ones do twice the work of the others, with no breakages, and (bless them!) leave all tidy afterwards. SECOND, they actually enjoy washing up. For it isn't the repetitiveness of a job which makes it boring, but inattention. THIRD, how much of our fear and pain come from importing into the present moment what doesn't belong to it! How much actual pain do we suffer at the dentist's? FOURTH, the long-term rewards of this training are serenity, detachment, self-knowledge. The more of ourselves we can bring to consciousness, the less it bugs us.

The FIFTH and chief reason for the practice of mindfulness is to graduate from *what's* being experienced to WHO's experiencing. In a word, enlightenment.

Theravada Buddhism insists on this long and hard preliminary training. It allows no short cuts to Nirvana. Rather discouraging for people like me, and I dare say like you, who are shy of paying such a price for what must be unknown goods! I'm mean, when it comes to buying such an expensive pig in a poke.

But let's take heart. There are other ways. The great Japanese Zen Master Ummon has words of comfort for us: "Zen places enlightenment *first*; get rid of your bad karma afterwards." Take delivery of your TV now, start viewing today, pay later. And what's specially attractive about this bargain offer is that the viewing is the paying! You get enlightened by doing it. Another great Master, Ramana Maharshi of Tiruvannamalai, never tired of telling his incredulous disciples that enlightenment or liberation is the easiest, simplest, most natural thing in the world: Who you really are is plainer than a fruit held in the palm of the hand.

Well, if the ultimate Awareness is as available as these and many other acknowledged experts claim it is, let's get it before we reach the end of these pages. No, I'm not having you on! Ten minutes should be more than enough.

Enlightenment (suprahuman) awareness

Allow me to direct your attention to your present experience, to how it is with you at this moment when (as far as possible) you drop memory and imagination and desire, and just take what's given. Will you please be childlike with me, just for a few minutes?

You are taking in a page covered with lines of black marks (these printed words), and held by two hands – of which the fingers are mostly not given. While continuing to look straight at this printing, notice how those two hands connect with arms that grow fuzzy and fade out altogether well short of your shoulders (what shoulders?). And now observe how, between these fuzzy arms stretches an area of chest which itself gets fuzzy and then disappears well short of any neck (what neck?). Try tracing with your finger now the "neckline" where your chest stops, and notice what's your side, the near side, of this permanent décolletage.

(Strange – isn't it? – how completely we overlook these near regions, refusing to see what we see where seeing matters most, and dishonesty is disaster.)

Another example: are you now, in your own first-hand experience, peering at these black marks through two (repeat, two) small windows in a globular, hairy look-out called a head? If so, kindly describe what it's like in there – congested? Dimly lit? Sticky? Small?

Or is it a fact that, *going by present evidence*, you find nothing whatever right here where you thought you sported a head, nothing but space? Space containing what? Space filled with these words, these pages, these arms and chest? Speckless and boundless capacity or room, alive to itself as empty – and filled with those things, taking in the ever-changing scene? Space, sometimes, for your face and head and shoulders also – where you find and keep them – over there behind your looking glass, quarter size, the "wrong" way round, and three feet adrift from your torso?

Yes, you've got it! You see with total clarity *Who* and what you've always been, namely this Disappearance in favour of others, this Emptiness which is aware of itself as no-thing and therefore all things. How could we not see this most obvious of all sights, once our attention is drawn to it?

Congratulations! You're enlightened! You always were.

But now comes the hard bit. Seeing what you really are is just about the easiest thing in the world to do, and just about the most difficult to keep doing – at first. Normally, it takes months and years and decades of coming back home, to the spot one occupies (or rather, doesn't occupy – the world does that) before one learns the knack of remaining centred, of staying indoors, of living from one's space instead of from one's face. Nevertheless, now you know how to get there, you can visit home whenever you wish and whatever your mood. And, once over the threshold, you're perfectly at home: here, you can't put a foot wrong. Practice doesn't *make* perfect here: it *is* perfect from the start. You can't half see your facelessness now, or see half of it. There are no degrees of enlightenment: it is all, or nothing.

Naturally there are many, many ways back to the home you never really left. Let me tell you about those which I find particularly useful. Among them you will find some that are right for you.

How to keep it up

Any face *there* is enough to dissolve the illusion of a face *here* above my shoulders, taking it in. How could I receive your face in all its colourful detail if it were blocked at this end by anything at all? I find I've never, never been face to face with anybody. This permanent asymmetry is the beginning of love and the end of fear. Imagining I've any shield or wall here to keep you out with is rejection of you, separation from and fear and even hatred of you. The remedy is to see that I'm built open, built for loving.

My mirror confirms this wide-openness right here where I am. The very thing which long ago put a face on me now relieves me of it. Now I look in the glass to see what I'm *not* like!

And if it occurs to me that all this is very visual, and that I can actually feel this solid thing here, filling up the *seeming* void at the centre of my world, why then I start stroking and pinching and pummelling this thing. Only to find it still isn't any thing at all, let alone a pink and white and hairy and opaque and all-together-in-one-piece thing. Instead, I find a succession of touch sensations that are no more substantial than the sounds and smells and tastes and so on, which also come and go in the same space.

And if I start wondering how on earth one could explain this to a blind person, why then I "go blind". Shutting my eyes (what eyes?) I start seeking my shape, my boundaries, my height and width, my sex… indeed all those things I'd identified with. And I discover that not a single one of them can be found now. I am still boundless space for sensations to occur in, alias silence for these passing sounds, alias no-mind entertaining this parade of thoughts and feelings. I'm nobody, cleaned out. Yet I feel no sense of loss. Quite the opposite: I'm aware of myself as unhurt, comfortable, relieved of a heavy load. It suits me just to *be*. I AM feels incomparably better than, more natural than, I AM SOMEBODY.

And if I suspect that it's not in passive contemplation but in action that I shall re-discover that missing somebody, why then I get on the move. Only to find I never move! It is the countryside that walks, jogs, runs, drives, dances through me. The space here is for things to move around in, not for moving. May I suggest you check this by standing up now and rotating on the spot. In your unedited experience, are *you* going round and round, or the *room*?

But how to reconcile that moving, headed, bounded, opaque human you take me to be, with my denial of all that? Who is right?

We're both right. What I amount to depends on where you're looking at me from. At six feet from this centre, you find a man. Approaching, you find a face, a patch of skin, and then (given the right instruments) tissues, cells, molecules… till, at the point of contact, I've vanished – and you confirm my view of myself right here. Or, retreating from this centre, you find a home, a city, a country, a planet, a star (the Solar System), a galaxy (the Milky Way); and again, in the limit, nothing at all. Your view of me, and my view of me, confirm and complement each other.

End of the dream

Well, having now seen your true Nature, and valuing what you see, you will find your own reminders to go on looking, till the looking becomes quite natural and effortless. Some of the experiments and pointers I've mentioned will surely work for you too. If you really want to live the aware life, to wake up from the social dream, to be Who you are, everything will spring to your aid and push you towards that supreme goal.

Attaining it is realising you never left it. Rather than *becoming* aware, you experience Awareness as your very being.

From My Hilltop

Denny Peat

My earliest memories of wondering 'what life was supposed to be about' were in my early teens. I found it hard to accept what other people told me. I had a nagging doubt about just who I was supposed to be, and it seemed at the time the more I asked the less I found out. To my surprise it wasn't a subject that many people wanted to discuss. Most people seemed perfectly happy not knowing, and just getting on with their lives. More than once I've thought, 'why can't I do that', but my need for meaning in my life has always surfaced. This led on to a lot of reading and I suppose the beginning of the journey that still goes on today.

In my early twenties I became involved with a group of people from a variety of backgrounds – students, parents, psychologists, carpenters, scientists – all searchers. We were involved in a project called 'The Centre for Human Communication'. At its heart was a model of personality based on the Chakra System. It is used as a way to understand the nature of personality and the different levels within it. At the time I found the work at the centre very fulfilling and I gained immensely from it. But still it wasn't enough, it didn't satisfy the searcher in me, it didn't answer a fundamental question: 'Who am I?' I gained a better understanding of my personality and others. I learned how to be more appropriate when dealing with different types of people, but there was still the question of 'who' it is that has this personality.

My search went on, sometimes intensely, sometimes almost forgotten. And then one day Tim, an old friend from the centre days was in our house talking with some other friends. I was busy doing something, but I caught the drift of what he was saying. Something about this old guy giving a talk at this Buddhist centre near to where we lived and how he was using some really simple experiments to show who we really are. I think it was the word simple that grabbed me. He told me he was doing a workshop at the weekend and did I fancy coming along. I decided to give it a go. I did the Saturday and to be honest I didn't get the point at all. By the end of the day I felt somewhat confused but something had touched me. I bought the book *On Having No Head* so I could look into it at my own pace. Well, I read it and I still didn't get what he was on about. But I knew he was on about something. I stayed up one night determined either to understand what he was on about or throw the book away. I remember sitting there in the small hours of the morning incredibly frustrated, thinking 'how can he say that? what does he mean?' And then I stood in front of a mirror and I suddenly got it. I saw what was in front of me (my head) and I saw this empty space where I always thought that my head was for me. I was shocked and also a little scared. How come I'd never noticed this before, it was so obvious. So simple. A thought ran through my head (if I could now say that!) – it was from the old centre days when I used to practice yoga, and someone would be leading a meditation, and they'd say something like 'I am in myself no thing'.

At the time I liked the sound of it but I didn't have a clue what it meant. Now I could see it for myself. A stream of partially understood ideas and concepts became instantly clear in the light of this experience.

In Memoriam

David Lang

O ne morning two years ago, I received a phone call from a woman wanting to meet people who were practising the Headless Way. She had been meditating for several years, and although she was quite familiar with the experience of Awareness, she said the people she had been meditating with didn't think they had had the experience themselves. Consequently, she felt isolated. Then she had come across one of Douglas's books, and realizing how shareable the Awareness could be, had contacted Douglas, who had given her my name and number.

I have rarely on the phone had such a strong sense of the I AM as I had that morning with Rebecca. She certainly wanted to talk about Awareness. But what was remarkable was how quickly the focus of the conversation shifted from the exchange of words about Being to the joint observation of those words arising from and disappearing into the vastness of Being. Here were two voices, ostensibly strangers to each other, sharing with immediacy their unity in the Self, recognizing in surprise and relief the familiarity underlying their separateness. Like bubbles in carbonated water, the voices rose from nowhere and then vanished again, expressions of the one listener/speaker who didn't have a clue as to what it was going to say to itself next. What a thrill it was to share this experience on the phone, out of the blue, with Rebecca.

One thing I learned about Rebecca during this conversation was that she had ovarian cancer. She was receiving chemotherapy, and her energy was affected greatly by both the cancer and the treatments. Sometimes, she said, she was exhausted, and sometimes, like this day, she felt fine. What impressed me, however, was the matter-of-fact way she shared what she was facing, not denying the fear that comes with having a life-threatening disease, yet not being drawn into the fear, either, but instead referring to herself in an unassuming manner as 'eternal Awareness'. And as our voices came and went like waves in the deathless ocean of Being, I appreciated how much of a resource Who we really are can be in times of need.

Over the next two years, Rebecca came quite often to the monthly meetings in the San Francisco Bay Area, enjoying with other people the direct sharing of Awareness and the spoken and unspoken acknowledgement that each person present saw fully Who he or she was. Her typical reaction to suggestions that we do experiments was to jump up and say, 'I'm ready'. And she brought to our discussions a maturity and focus, couched in an easy-going manner, which I missed when she did not come to a meeting.

Gradually, Rebecca came less and less to the meetings, not because she lacked interest but because the cancer and the chemotherapy were taking away her energy. I would call her, and we would talk about our Identity, and I would put the phone down feeling inspired. But one day, after a couple of months of being out of touch, I called her and heard a message in a stranger's voice which referred me to another number in Southern California. Rebecca, I learned from her friend at that number, had died in peace some weeks before, at home, surrounded by loving friends.

What do you do when a friend dies? How do you make meaning out of his or her absence? I am sure there are as many ways of dealing with someone's death as there are people affected by it. But in the next monthly meeting, after I had shared the circumstances of her death, we did a lovely thing. We gathered together, arms around each other, and looking down into the center of the circle, did the 'No-head Circle' experiment in honor of Rebecca. A voice, falling out of and into the Emptiness, began:

'Down there on the carpet we see a circle of feet, feet of friends who have come today to be together, feet of friends who will later leave, going off in different directions. Down there is the land of feet, the land of separate comings and goings, of hellos and goodbyes, of births and deaths. And into this land, Rebecca will not come again. We are saying our last goodbye to you, Rebecca, and giving you our love as you take the next step in your journey. Thank you for your presence here, for your energy and wisdom. We wish you well, Rebecca. Goodbye.

'But here, up here at the top of the circle of bodies, still looking down, we find no feet, nor heads, nor separate no-heads, no land of comings and goings, births and deaths, hellos followed by goodbyes. Here, in this unfathomable presence, in the midst of these few bodies gathered together, is the I AM, silently voicing, when we care to look, the eternal, timeless Hello of Who we really are. And here too, in the midst, free of the distinctions that separate you from me, is Rebecca - the real Rebecca, who so steadfastly lived from Who she really was - the real Rebecca and the real you and the real me. Rebecca, hello.'

Now other voices appear and disappear, like birds flying across this sky of Awareness, evoking memories and images of Rebecca, last seen in this room. How present she feels amongst us now, how real. And how beautiful it is to spend together this time remembering her and wishing her well.

The voices cease. We absorb ourselves in the depthless, deathless Awareness. And then, slowly, we look up, taking in now the circle of faces of friends present. A face is missing. Whose? It is the face of the One who has died and been reborn into eternal life.

At some level, I suspect, someone else's death is our own death. We grieve the death of the other, and in that grieving we also grieve our own approaching death. Yet we can also see in that person's absence the Absence which is our own, the Absence which is also Presence. In Rebecca's life, and death, and Life, I find my own.

Nowhere To Go

Richard Lang

There is no end to our willing and longing until we know God in the fullness of joy.

JULIAN OF NORWICH (C. 1342 – 1413)

I haven't meditated for some time. But I am awake at 5:30am – wide-awake. So I get up and, having lit a candle in the living room, sit on a cushion and close my eyes. For a few minutes I am waiting for something to happen, waiting to drop down into stillness, into peace and fulfilment. Waiting to let go. Suddenly I realise that everything I am searching for is here, already present, already fulfilled. Unbreakable peace is my nature. Utter stillness is my being. God is present fully where I am and am not – nearer to me than my jugular vein (as the Koran so graphically puts it). Everything the greatest mystics speak so passionately about – I mean the essential, simplest, deepest things – is here at my centreless centre. I am that living, wild, outrageous sea…

I am both familiar with and astonished by this truth. Sighing I let go. I am empty of myself. What relief and freedom. Nowhere to go, nothing to achieve, no-one to be. Here in nothingness all is received, from the furthest galaxy to the nearest particle – no distance! Here from emptiness all is released – and taken care of – from my own personal worries to wider and deeper concerns. And here in silence all is as it should be. Or as Julian of Norwich said, 'All shall be well, and all shall be well, and all manner of things shall be well.' I know what she was talking about. I feel a profound relaxation – physical and psychological. I fall back into nothingness. Quiet joy rises in my heart, inspiration flows, peace deepens, freedom declares itself unashamed and true.

I honour this bottomless truth, invisibly bowing down to the marvel of my innermost outermost being. I take a deeper breath. Breathing out I open my eyes, the shapes of the room springing forward into the undivided openness of my edgeless single eye. The growing light of day is creeping into the room, chasing away the night. I gaze for a few moments at the burning candle – looking from lightless nothingness into the vulnerable shimmering flame. Fire flickers in stillness.

Then, grateful and at peace, I rise from my cushion, blow out the candle, and make breakfast.

From The Withered Tree A Flower Blooms

Peter Janson-Smith

My practice needs to return, again and again, to the basics. Just what exactly am I looking out of? What precisely do I outline when I caress the edges of this Single Eye with my finger tips? I can find nothing closer to me than this infinitely elastic Window. Yet one glance is enough to see that this frameless Window is actually framed by the six directions. Hence, looking in the outward direction, this Window is the objects it holds. Looking in the inward direction, this Window holds nothing but Nothing. The easterly and westerly directions fade away into this Nothing. The upward and downward directions also make contact with the Void. Indeed, I have only to look up and down to find that my world is always bounded by two distinct lines where the world gives way to No-world. The Top Line can be called the Transcendent God as it cradles the sky and the stars or whatever else it happens to be smiling down on. The Bottom Line may be called the Immanent God as it always underlies the field of the world, and is most often found beneath my chest. If I really look, both the Transcendent God and the Immanent God become one at my back, as my backing.

Meanwhile, now that I see where I'm coming from, I can go on to play the human game with less compulsion and more fun. Invariably, I find I can be more human when I'm seeing/being the game-free nucleus of that human life. Moreover, seeing improves my capacity to feel my life, to experience with compassion exactly those emotions that I reject, exactly those emotions our culture rejects as too ugly, too selfish, too embarrassing, too small, too mean, too humiliating. Seeing allows us to feel our existence without feeling trapped. It allows us to do what Keats exhorted us all to do: 'feel your life, thrive on its mess and struggles'. Consciously seeing that which we are, renders us more available to our lives. They say that tolerance for our weaknesses is a fundamental prerequisite to healing. Well, looking in now, I see that I contain those weaknesses as expressions of the depths of my nature. Seeing guides us to what we have been avoiding and gives us the courage to live that line in the Shoyo Roku: 'From the withered tree, a flower blooms'.

My Special Friend

Douglas Harding

Mother and I are looking out of the oval window at the children playing.
'What are their names?' I ask.
'That's Johnny, the one with the black hair. The one with her back to us is Mary Anne. The other one is You Darling.'
'That's a funny name. Why does he keep staring? Why doesn't he play outside the other windows sometimes?'
'Because he is You Darling.'
'Does having that name make him stare at me? I think it's because he's my special friend.'
The years pass. Johnny and Mary Anne have gone.
But my friend is always there outside the oval window,
like a good yard dog who knows he isn't allowed indoors.
Sometimes he's full of fun, sometimes miserable
but he never takes his eyes off me.
Now he's growing old and grey and slow, and often sad looking.
I think he's begging to be let in.
I think that if I let him in he would be all over me, smothering me.
He might even kill me, kill me with kindness.
And because he loves me so much, when he dies he wants me to go with him.
If I let my friend in he will be my enemy.
I will not let him in.

Figuring Out The Unfiguroutable

David Lang

The story of the Prodigal son, as interpreted by Douglas Harding, is a clear description of our journey out to the far land of the mirror and then back again to our real nature. But I am sure that the son, after the feast and celebrations were over and he had begun to work again for his father, suffered the effects of a clash between the new world-view of his Home and the old world-view he had got used to in the far country. I imagine, as Douglas suggests for us all in *On Having No Head*, that there was for the Prodigal Son a long period of working out the significance of being Home again.

In my own life, the celebration that came on being shown that I was, like Traherne, 'the sole heir of the whole world' who was 'clothed with the heavens, and crowned with the stars' has been followed by years of trying to resolve differences between what I learned to think in the far country and what I now see in the near country. And a central question I have tried to answer for myself during this time has been: Are other people conscious?

In the far country, that would be an unthinkable, ridiculous, even dangerous question. There, respect for others is founded on the principle that people are separate, conscious individuals. The idea that one had a monopoly on consciousness would be considered, at the very least, narcissistic. In the first 'Headless' workshop I attended, however, the principle was challenged, for I perceived that people did not possess their own, separate consciousnesses. Indeed, they didn't seem conscious at all. I remember looking at a man across the circle of people doing experiments, noticing how his spectacled, lined face was beautifully on display in my No-face, and realizing that his face, indeed his whole appearance, was two-dimensional. I looked around the circle, and the people appeared to me like child-size, cardboard cutouts on display in the window of my Seeing. They were all as colorful and as animated as before, but their eyes didn't see like my single Eye saw, and their heads were too small to contain anything - brains, minds, or souls. Apparently, while I had lost my head and found Consciousness in its place, they had kept their heads but had lost their consciousnesses. My becoming sole heir of the whole world had disinherited everyone else.

The idea that people weren't conscious, that behind them was nothing, that they were just appearances, ciphers, things in the world, worried me a lot. At best this was solipsism; at worst it was a recipe for totalitarian disrespect. And yet, confusingly, this perception that eyes did not see was accompanied by a refreshing openness and respect. One of my strongest memories from that time of Homecoming is of looking, relieved of self-consciousness by my own absence, into the loving and relaxed eyes of a new 'headless' friend.

'Headless' friend? Here was another confusion. For while we agreed in the workshop that, on present evidence, no consciousness resided in the eyes of the people around us, we cheerfully accepted each person's patently untrue assertion that he or she was headless and was the dwelling-place of infinite Awareness.

I was all mixed up, trying to hold two conflicting positions at the same time: my perception that people were not conscious and my belief that people were infinitely Conscious. Furthermore, this belief that people were Conscious got confused with the idea that people had separate consciousnesses. As a result, I went around thinking vaguely that there were two types of Consciousness: mine, which was infinite and obvious; and other people's, which were infinite and yet hidden somehow somewhere over there, one in each person's center, but also blending together with other consciousnesses in a kind of infinitely clear soup behind people's appearances.

So the return Home raised questions that I needed to work out. Are people conscious? If I believe they are, then I am disregarding what I perceive, and the idea of sharing Seeing - presumably some kind of transmission between voids that are not separate - is an awkward one. On the other hand, if I go with my perception that people are not conscious, what is the point of sharing 'head-lessness' with cardboard cutouts who have heads, and why is it rewarding to do so?

The answers to these questions, such as can be expressed, were there for the looking.

I sit on my back step looking out. Late afternoon sunshine fills the high blue sky; the leaves on the trees thrill in the wind; fence and flowers and lawn seem to relax after the hot day. I look at the trees. I see with surprise that no thing sees them blowing in the wind. That which is doing the looking has absolutely no qualities, no divisions within itself, no inside or outside, no here or there. It is so empty that it isn't even an 'it', has no identity at all. And yet, with nothing going for it, it sees the trees and the sky and the house next door. Naked of me, mysterious, no-thing is conscious.

Conscious - not only of the garden but also of its own emptiness. No-thing is miraculously aware of itself as no-thing! And the Consciousness does not stop there. The emptiness is also aware that its own empty Awareness has no source, that it comes impossibly from nowhere, like lamplight shining without a lamp. Here is indefinable Consciousness arising out of absolute Unconscious-ness. No room is left anywhere for other Consciousnesses, finite or infinite. The idea of separate awarenesses won't stand up. Consciousness is alone.

And all the time, not a hairsbreadth separating it from this Consciousness, the garden enjoys the sunshine.

A few days later I stand at the top of a staircase in a large grocery store, looking out over the crowd of small, two-dimensional shoppers. I perceive no Consciousness inside or behind them. And then the obvious hits me smack in the face. How silly I've been, trying to imagine hidden Consciousnesses in other people or supposing that people are not conscious. They are conscious, but their Consciousness is in front of them, not behind or within them. It is all over the store! It couldn't be more real or less hidden. This infinitely awake No-thing, which has no here or there, no inside or outside, no other to compare, is their Consciousness just as it is mine and no-one's. What a surprise, like coming by chance upon one's closest friend in a foreign country. This is you! This is you! I pick out a face in the crowd, and I stare at our open Identity. I find another face and do the same. The Consciousness of each is not separate. There are no dividing lines. The people in the store are all walking around in this shared Consciousness, which is neither mine nor theirs and yet is them and me, like fish swimming around in water.

And so, with Traherne, I come to see that I enjoy the world aright when I am not only perceiving myself to be 'the sole heir of the whole world' but also seeing in it people 'who are every one sole heirs' as well as me.

Furthermore, my enjoyment of the world includes sharing consciousness, for seeing it is sharing it. Whether we acknowledge it or not, 'we' enjoy the oneness of Being. When the Prodigal Son returns Home, all the guests at the feast are also Home. And yet when the conversation turns directly to the acknowledgement that we are at Home, and we toast and celebrate that fact, self-awareness takes on a special quality. A friend and I talk on the phone about how we are not two people talking on the phone. Instead, 'we' hear two bodiless voices appearing out of and disappearing into one Awareness, like airborne motes of dust shining in sunlight for a moment. Two voices, but one speaker-listener who is somehow more easily aware of being the one consciousness as 'we' notice together our Absence.

So, have I worked out satisfactory answers to my question? Are other people conscious, and does the idea of sharing 'Headlessness' now make sense? Well, yes and no. I certainly don't feel the original confusion around these particular questions. In fact, the opposite. But I also realize that, while it is necessary and inspiring to figure out the meaning of being Home, it is in the end and the beginning unfiguroutable. Being Home is a mystery which is opaque to thought but which has nothing to hide from the simple eye of looking.

Praise To Lalla

Richard Lang

Dance, Lalla, with nothing on
but air. Sing, Lalla,
wearing the sky.

Look at this glowing day! What clothes
could be so beautiful, or
more sacred?

LALLA (14th CENTURY)

Born in Kashmir, Lalla wandered and danced naked as she sang. Her songs flowed from her living experience of God, from her true being which is our true being.

I am imagining Lalla walking down a country road. She is awake to the clarity of her own infinite being, an emptiness that is room for sky and earth and all things in between. Transparent like pure water, lighter than air, the world dances within her. Those leaves trembling in the breeze, these stones on the dry road, this brown mud by the lazy river – she puts them all on like clothes. An ever-changing wardrobe. To be one thing only, to wear your face, your body, as yourself, is no longer to have room for anything else. But to be naked, to be the absolute openness of being – then are we richly attired. I am reminded of the German mystic Meister Eckhart (who died when Lalla was probably about seven): 'As long as I am this or that, I am not all things.' I think too of the seventeenth century English poet Traherne: 'You never enjoy the world aright till the sea itself floweth in your veins, till you are clothed with the heavens and crowned with the stars…'

And so, Lalla, with nothing on you dance in the tumbling mountain stream, in swans gliding on glistening waters, in the laughing children playing about your feet. And as you dance you sing, Lalla, oh how you sing. Praise overflows from the well-spring of nothing, from the mystery within – an endless song to God, from God.

Today, Lalla, I find your body everywhere. I see you in the faces of everyone I meet, I taste you in the drink I lift to my lips, I hear you in the crackling fire and in the silent earth, in the cacophony of sounds on city streets, in waves breaking ever new on wide beaches. The stars gaze down with your eyes, Lalla, the bird in flight beats the air with your wings, the flower with petals open to the sun is your beautiful face. Wherever I look I find you. You who are without are within, my side of every door on which I knock.

Lalla, in the unplanned flow of my own hands and feet when I dance, I unfold in your dance. Reaching out to another, I touch you. Taking off the clothes of my own appearance I am joined with you.

(Poem from *Naked Song*, Lalla, translated by Coleman Barks, published by Maypop.)

Creating Space

Jochen Encke

It was last spring that I came across Richard Lang's workshop The Headless Way. It was quite an experience that with a few simple techniques our reality, or what we believe our reality is about, can be blown apart.

But this was not the main reason why this workshop was so exciting for me. Some days after the workshop I suddenly remembered an incident I had in my early twenties, about twenty years ago.

I remember sitting on the roof of my VW bus watching a group of about fifteen people talking to each other. I think we were about to join some sort of political march. I was very relaxed. I smoked a cigarette and with one breath I inhaled a bit of the cigarette smoke. As I was not a smoker this one breath made me a bit dizzy. I had done that before. But this time something happened which would become very special to me: I suddenly lost my head. I looked down at my body, which I could definitely see, but I could not see my head. To my surprise it was not frightening at all, it did not feel empty up there. I felt like an oversized magnifying glass, the handle was my body, the glass was where my head used to be – and somebody was looking through it at the group of people below my bus. There were no thoughts interfering because there was no head. I was just watching – but was it actually me who was watching? I remember my confusion. I definitely felt empty and a mere channel. Something, somebody, was holding the lower part of my body like I would hold the handle of a magnifying glass, and looking through it – through my empty space where I thought the upper part of my body was supposed to be. But I also was this something or somebody who was looking through it. I felt an intense warmth for the world and a happiness I had never experienced before.

But would you believe it? I forgot this experience soon after it. Why? Because I had no space in myself to store it. It is a bit like the way I sometimes deal with my paperwork. If I do not know under which label or on which part of my shelf I ought to put it, I just throw it away.

The workshop provided me with a label. It demanded a new space on my 'inner shelf' which consequently started filling up very quickly. This usually happens when we create space. Nature does not like emptiness. Emptiness draws energy. And that is exactly what happened. Other memories appeared and, what is more important, new experiences of this sort started occurring much more frequently. Maybe I catch them more easily, or maybe I have just created a space for them to happen in.

Rose Gardens Within Rose Gardens

Richard Lang

If you pass beyond form, O friends, it is Paradise and rose-gardens within rose-gardens.
When you have broken and destroyed your own form, you have learned to break the form of everything.

RUMI (1207 – 1273)

It's Saturday night and I'm at a party with friends. I love dancing and barely stop moving the whole evening long. Music drenches the air, a downpour without pause till we're soaked to the skin. Now I dance with this friend, now with that one, now with someone I've never met before. And in the midst of this spinning room of whirling dervishes I'm awake to the stillness of being, and the stillness moves me, guides me, leads me on and on, deeper into the dance. Drinking from this well of nothingness that is my source always present I become drunk, yet still I drink, addicted to this nectar. Diving down deep into the wild ocean I watch you bursting forth into new life and yet, though I drown in life-giving waters still I dive, deeper and deeper, into the dark unknown. This fire within has consumed me, burned me away without trace but I cannot stop, feeding more wood and breath into the hot blaze till orange flames dance still more fiercely and I die again, and again rise like a phoenix from grey ashes into shining day. What joy and freedom to be bodiless again as if for the first time, like a child, to be invisible and innocent, dissolved into emptiness that miracles into being as this dancing body, these dancing friends. Light as air, clear as water, wide as the sky, the party is alive within me. As the beat drives on, into the early hours, I hear the silence inside – music that never ends.

Now I'm dancing with another friend, taking in her open face, her laughing eyes, flowing with and around and against the sparkling stream and river and torrent she is tonight – now playful, now serious, now close, now distant. How wonderful to be free of my own face now, my own body here, shape-shifting into unspeakable formlessness, wide open for two bodies weaving new patterns, empty for two selves rooted in mystery. I breathe, letting go into indivisible being, into this dance now. What fun so to move with another, not knowing where we're bound, inspired by the song, possessed by the rhythm, feeling our feet and the ground conversing, riding wild waves that rise and break and crash down and rise again. Nothing here to be or know, nothing here to protect, nothing here to have or hold onto, no surface or boundary keeping her out. Transparent, uncontained, I include the two of us. Marvellous and bright emptiness, full of fresh beauty.

Break through the shell of your own appearance and the boundlessness that reveals itself belongs to everyone, embraces everyone, is everyone's birthright. Rumi found rose-gardens. Tonight I find friends loving dancing, and between me and them no distance at all.

CORRESPONDENCE FROM
SEEING FRIENDS

These emails have been collected over the last five years (1998 – 2003) and provide insights into the way seeing who you really are affects people. Most of this correspondence took place in a discussion group on the internet.

Since I was a child, I have always been troubled by feelings of embarrassment, especially when I had to speak in public. This reached its 'summit' when I was about 14 years old. When I had to address more than three people, I just could not utter one syllable. In Dutch we call this 'spreekangst' (literally translated 'fear of speaking'). This became better when I got older, but it never really disappeared. About one and a half years ago I had to give a speech. I forgot about two thirds of what I wanted to say, just because of these feelings of embarrassment. I now remember that Douglas Harding, in one of his books, talked about something similar which he experienced when he was young.

Last year, during the holidays, I was attending a workshop with Douglas in the Ardeche. I was amazed that I did not feel the slightest bit of embarrassment when I had to do the experiments, and even speaking in public was no problem. Especially the experiment with the tube made me feel comfortable with the whole group.

Nowadays, these problems have almost disappeared. Every time I have to speak in public, I focus on the public itself, on what I have to say and also on the Void they are looking at, instead of focusing on 'how will they think about me (that means, the image I have of myself), will they find me odd and so on...' At the same time, I have to say that this does not mean that Douglas gave me an efficient 'trick' or something, because when you focus too much on results, it won't work. And this is true for the whole of Douglas's 'teaching'. You just have to do the experiments to see, but when you start doing the experiments with expectations of enlightenment, mystic experience, of becoming a person who is completely without problems and complexes and so on, they won't work. This makes me think of something Krishnamurti said: 'Each "attempt" to meditate is the denial of meditation.' Just seeing, observing who you really really are, is the meditation. And this includes dropping all ideas of becoming enlightened, self-assured and so on.

Marc

My name is Jeremy and I'm living in Amsterdam, although I am English. I came across the headless way about three years ago when I attended a two-day seminar Douglas gave near Nice, in the South of France. The finger-pointing exercise literally blew my head away, and the closed-eye one finished me off. I hadn't expected anything from the seminar. The name Douglas Harding was familiar: I had read something about him in a book by Colin Wilson called *Beyond the Occult*. Wilson quotes the famous passage from the beginning of *On Having No Head* and then goes on to say that that's all very well but it's probably the kind of emptiness and simplicity experienced by cows in a field! Well, I thought, perhaps I was in for an entertaining lecture on Zen Buddhism. I was in no way expecting to be literally decapitated. It was difficult not to burst out in peals of laughter during the rest of the seminar. That night, and every night for about the next three weeks, I found the in-seeing – awareness of oneself – to be so interesting and absorbing, so perfect and complete, that going to sleep seemed an absurdity. I lay awake for hours – just staying with the seeing and the realisation of what this all means.

Since then, seeing has become less intense but has remained constant. It took a little while to 'get' the assertion that it is the world and not I that moves. Now it's a tremendous thing to cycle around this beautiful city and see, beyond all doubt, that it's Amsterdam that flies by while 'I' am this awake unmoving stillness. The way close objects like the road beneath one's feet flash by and more distant things like buildings and trees float past gracefully is a spectacle I never tire of. This has certainly become my favourite exercise.

Jeremy

We did the experiment in which you point at yourself, and spin around your own axis. This reminded me of an experience I have with aikido (a martial art). Two or three times a week I practice aikido. At some moments, I had two difficulties during my practice: one was that, when I trained with some people, I felt a kind of fear when somebody 'attacked' me, so that my body became tense and stiff, which hindered carrying out the technique. Another problem was that I sometimes became dizzy, because there is a lot of tumbling around in aikido. These problems vanished into thin air when I reminded myself of the Void I am. When somebody attacked me, I felt relaxed, because who was there to be attacked? When I had to tumble around I did not feel dizzy anymore, because there was no one here to feel dizzy. And besides, there was only a stillness in which the world turned around, not me.

Marc

The question 'How do others who "see" deal with life's difficult situations?' makes me want to react. Last year I went to hospital to have a malignant melanoma (skin cancer) removed. Since skin cancer is the most lethal kind of cancer among younger people and since I am in my mid-thirties, I understood the physical risk was serious. During the weeks before the operation I went through different stages mentally. I remember very well how I was walking in town one summer day, seeing all those different people's faces. I started feeling more and more depressed, thinking: 'You can all live on for years and years to come, and I may not even be here anymore when the year 2000 starts.' I sank away in these thoughts, especially disliking people who looked 'too' happy.

Then, during one clear, merciful moment, I suddenly realised where all those faces as well as those depressing thoughts were taking place: right here, in Me. Gradually my mood changed from depression to all-including happiness. I saw many more different faces that day, but now I felt so much love for them; they were all stars in my universe and I was the One to enjoy their beauty. I 'myself' was gone and with it all the depressing thoughts. I did no longer complain with 'Why is this happening to me?' It was so clear that anything always 'happens' to Me, or rather in Me. Everything that is experienced, by 'anyone', is only experienced in Me. That is probably why I started feeling a pleasant, warm kind of pity for people as well. If something nasty happens to someone 'else', I see very clearly that this other person is to him- or herself nothing but Me, too. And when this person does not realise this, I feel this pity, or rather, compassion, for him or her. I empathise with the feelings he or she experiences in this situation, and meanwhile I see the situation does not really happen to that person, but is seen in his or her essence, his or her Me-ness, right here in consciousness.

During the rest of the weeks before my operation and during my stay in the hospital, relatives and friends were very kind to me, but quite a few of them needed my comfort more than I needed theirs. I had no fear of dying anymore, because 'my' death would mean nothing but 'their' death - the death of their appearance as human beings. Since for me, it is more and more like I do not have a personal past, I see fewer possible heavy losses on this side of life when I die. Moreover, death is the last adventure I will experience, so whenever it comes, let's go for it!

Going for it... For me it is becoming clear that this is what a truly happy life comes down to. Not in an active, 'doing' sort of way, but in the 'totally letting come and go' way.

Han

I first read *On Having No Head* about 20 years ago. At the time I was much too complicated and looking for 'big' things to really see what Douglas meant. This past year, after working intensively with some books (one especially helpful example is Thomas Cleary's translation of *The Golden Flower*, which is all about 'turning the light around'), I began having occasional flashes of headlessness, which called to mind Douglas's book, but only in a very general way. I worked in whatever ways I could figure out to encourage the experience, and finally one day came across a copy of *No Head* in a bookshop.

This time, when I read it, I saw just what was meant, and was able to answer for the first time a nagging koan-like question that had been chasing me ever since the time (again, about 20 years ago) it descended on me. I was a taxi driver at the time, and had fallen asleep at a cabstand. I suddenly awoke, aware of nothing but snowflakes against a black sky, and the question of why there was Anything instead of Nothing. On the heels of this came a more worrying question: If there were just Nothing at all, where would(n't) it be? Well, upon this recent re-reading of Douglas's book, I realized that the Where in question is of course Right Here, where I am. I thereupon had that happy experience I suspect is familiar to all of you, i.e., racing back through passages of favourite books and teachings, seeing them in a 'new light' and mostly laughing at the simple obviousness of it all.

In closing, I will offer two little exercises of my own. The first exercise would only be useful to anyone who might share my hobby/vice of long-distance bicycle riding. I've noticed that when I become tired, it's mostly a psychological manifestation that springs from using mental energy to 'project' myself forward through space, from one village to another, as if my mind believes it is accomplishing the work. As an antidote, I simply look down for a moment, instead of 'ahead', and what do I see? A stationary bicycle, with some legs going round in a circle, and pavement speeding by underneath. But I'm not going anywhere, of course, and there's nothing to be tired about.

I also tried this walking down the street, when I realized that even in walking I was projecting myself mentally from one point to some destination, whereas it's perfectly possible and infinitely richer and more enjoyable to walk along with a perception of one's stationary essence and let the world go by, as it were.

Thomas

My professional work in composition seems permanently punctuated by an amateur's sense of awe as I contemplate the mystery of creativity from a seeing perspective – where in the world are these notes emerging from? Who is doing this? (Usually I just get on with it, without much spiritual contemplation, but that sense of awe and mystery is never too far from the surface.)

If I have any problem in seeing, it is not with regard to my 1st-person experience, which is very clear, but in remembering that there is a 3rd-person Jan, invisible to me but visible to others. When I'm addressing a choir, I see before me a great sea of singers with No Conductor Here! But I must remind them to watch me, to listen to me – and must remind myself, 'For them, there is something here.' It is sometimes a little difficult to take on faith one's 3rd person-hood, to be responsible and authoritative about something that, from here, is absent! My students have just given me their farewells and acknowledgements at the end of the year, and again, when they tell me what an influence I was on their development, how I affected them, what an impact I had, it's sometimes difficult to get it. They're talking about something – someone – that isn't in your

1st-person experience, and you have to restrain yourself from shouting at them, 'But there's no one here!'

Although I have many good non-seer friends who understand me on most matters, this is one matter which only you guys and other Douglas friends can comprehend. A non-seer, misunderstanding what I said above, would say, 'You put yourself down; you don't give yourself credit for what you do.' And they'd say that even louder if you retorted, 'I am Nothing!'

Thanks to you all for understanding this central matter!

Jan

Two-way looking is a good way to put it. Let me give an example of something that happened to me last week. I woke up in the night feeling very thirsty, so I got up and went to the sink and poured myself a glass of water. I brought the water up to my mouth, and poured – straight into a void. The water disappeared. I was aware of my image in the mirror with a glass of water at the lips of that face, and I was aware of the water disappearing into a void. Perhaps because it was quiet and the middle of the night it all seemed especially clear.

Mara

I just wanted to share with you this extraordinary experience. As I started to attend yoga classes regularly (twice a day) to counteract involvement with a full-time job, a remarkable thing happened. The body almost automatically shifts into states of profound stillness. A window opens from within and I am literally being pulled into seeing.

These states became very spontaneous and intense. Last night this transparent vast Presence loomed over from within as an unmistakable fact. It was containing my body and the entire room within. The experience was so stunning that all thoughts scattered away. The reality of this non-material monstrously vast Density at the very core of my being made me speechless.

No wonder some people after ultimate enlightenment, fell into silence, mouna. Thoughts and involvements flee when their master wakes up, one-eyed, self-luminous.

Elena

I'd like to tell you guys about a neat experience with headlessness at a business meeting I ran over the last two days.

It was our yearly Strategic Planning Meeting - 'we' are a fairly large Energy sector Engineering/Construction company. There were sixteen senior managers, the VP and Chairman and me - the most junior person. I was the 'facilitator' and essentially I was running the meeting. A potentially stressful event like this can bring out insecure (or pushy) behaviour in me, but I'm learning humility slowly over the past many years.

Whenever I started to assert myself, things went downhill. Whenever I receded into quietness ('letting them get on with it') things went downhill. The knack is being humble and confident (I expect I'm reporting lessons many of you have learnt long ago).

Anyway, I was going into 'headless space' from time to time as a better place to operate from, but the striking thing happened at lunch. I experienced them as 'in me', a factual observation, but real, nice... and effective. We had the best planning meeting we've ever had and 'I' (the one without a head) was complimented on how I managed the meeting.

This headless stuff is as insubstantial as air, yet equally useful.

Andrew

The coyotes were howling last night, the mosquitoes whining. I looked for my nohead and I couldn't find it. Where has my nohead gone? It used to be my favourite thing!

Andrew

I read an article by Douglas about 25 years ago. It made a big impression but I heard no more for another 20 years. I then heard him being interviewed, late one Thursday night, on a Sydney radio station. In the meantime, I had been busy exploring various avenues including Zen, Krishnamurti and the Christian mystics. I am particularly keen on Traherne. As a result of the radio programme, I attended a lecture by Douglas the following day, then a seminar at the weekend. The pointing finger did the trick and I was amazed and delighted to find that what had previously only happened accidentally or infrequently after extensive preparation, was so simple, obvious and readily available.

Alan

I was experiencing an occasion of personal crisis at the time, and I was loaned *On Having No Head* by a friend. Reading it completely changed my way of being. But it was a very difficult time. I didn't understand fully what had happened. 'Who am I? Who is this that is seeing? And if there is no "me", what's all this? (indicating environment). If there's no subject, how can there be objects?' It was a very painful time - not all the bliss and joy that I read about in *The Headless Way*. That was 1975. I recently described it as initiating an enquiry into the-one-who-is-seeing-but-can't-be-seen. I suppose that says it.

Then, in 1979, I went to England to attend talks by Krishnamurti at Brockwood, and after that was over I went to London. As headlessness was still the dominant theme of my life, I decided to track down Douglas. It was simple: a visit to the London Buddhist Society, a phone call to Nacton, and off I went.

Douglas invited me to stay overnight, and so I had the opportunity to see It with him. (I must admit he looked at me with suspicion a couple of times, 'cause I was a bit off the planet, but he was kind and, seemingly, patient.)

Then - when was it? 1992? I'm not sure - Douglas came out here to Australia and I attended a two-day workshop. Confirmation time. The-one-that-sees-is unsee-able. It was then that I mentioned that after reading his book, I couldn't ever believe again that I was a little someone on the inside looking out, but that I'd had 17 years of difficulties due to this. He said: 'Yes, the little man doesn't give up easily.' All that pain summed up so simply, but he was right! That's all it's been.

Formally speaking, I practice Zen, being an inheritor of a lineage and all, but the heart of my 'practice', or what I always come back to, when the chips are down, is headlessness.

Chris

Instinctively I don't think one has to go through stages anymore than a cat or a baby goes through stages to realise I AM. A baby or a cat just IS - no stages or levels to it. We were babies once, too, and had the same realisation, but then forgot about it and learned to identify with our little separate selves. So, it is more a question of relaxed unlearning than striving to change focus. Remembering who I really am often seems to occur to me as I drive to work and see my Self still and the road moving through Me. I don't think that you can conceptualise or think your way there - just look and see. The question is how to remember to look and see - and I think, after the initial seeing, that one returns naturally to drink at this Oasis, because we thirst for it. You go back when you're thirsty.

Mara

I encountered the seeing experiments in Mr. Harding's workshops here in Maui, Hawaii, in 1989. The experience then, and since then, was no sudden new revelation, but a gradual clarifying confirmation of intuitions infrequently noticed since childhood: intuitions I had learned were called the Perennial Wisdom - that some basic aspect of our experience here and now was touching the infinite and eternal.

The clarifying and confirming may be helped along by the experiments, or not. My first impression of them in 1989 was mixed. I admired their simplicity, 'down to earth-ness', and humour. Reflections of Mr. Harding's enthusiastic personality, I remember thinking. On the other hand I was concerned that they could be rather easily dismissed as based on apparently superficial or childish tricks of perception. At any rate, the import of them was clearly to 'in-point' to our nature as spirit in a harmlessly entertaining sincerely felt way.

Things were left at that for two or three years. Then in 1992 I read *Head Off Stress*, and interest in this approach to our True Identity grew. The book's pragmatic topic and approach was quite compelling. I read what other material by Mr. Harding I could find locally. I started to 'practice' - to focus on an experiment a day for a five or six day series, such as the exercise program at the back of *Head Off Stress*. I shared experiments occasionally, quite casually with one or two people at a time. I introduced them as a 'simple, down-to-earth way of seeing what Ramana Maharshi, or Nisargadatta, or the Buddhists, or whoever, was talking about'. Reactions ranged from 'Yes, that's a nice simple way of putting it' to 'Oh really? Is that all?'

How has seeing affected me? Does it make a difference? Things, people, places seem more interesting, revitalised, available. It's a relief that I can and do live more efficiently as conscious 1st person than as the assumed, rather exasperating, familiar yet unruly 3rd person I was overseeing. Experience is here, not slightly off at an alienating distance in memory or imagination, so living regains more of a childlike innocence in its lighter, simpler feel. In comparison, not-seeing feels like living in a dark burdensome place, like the cave of Plato's allegory.

For me headlessness is not a void or felt absence-of-a-head, but seeing that a head here is just naturally out of the picture in favour of a kind of clarity to whatever's on show. It's certainly not an achievement or a means to an end or a technique; it's just good to see what really is the case, how I really do live. Achievements and techniques may then follow, or not.

And seeing is instantaneous and timeless, though it certainly takes time to follow up all the implications, to let it make a difference, to live it. For instance, one can see the Hierarchy in a moment: up are the stars, out are the hills and city lights, down is one's hand with its cells and molecules and atoms, further down one's arm is the Bottom Line and...? The observer and the observed obviously belong together in seeing this. But to live from this vision would be to live from the fact that humanity and the earth are one, which would surely mean big socio-economic and political changes from how we live now.

Something I have been working/playing with is how seeing contrasts with what traditional psychology advises on managing our thoughts and feelings and our relationships. It's unconventional but often effective in my experience to let 'my' thoughts and feelings that seem to float around here in 'me' instead migrate back to their appropriate objects 'out there', and then perhaps to see that after all they and their objects are Here! That I'm empty of all things and also chock-full of them, as the head-shaped hole in the card experiment demonstrates. And then I can act towards the thoughts instead of reacting from them, as Stephen Levine puts it. This approach can be a lot simpler and more fun than ponderous analytical psychology, but I can't begin to say just when and where each style is appropriate. But I do know that relationships take on an altogether different feeling when it is seen that I can't help but take in that one's face, words, touch. In this sense alienation is simply impossible. Spontaneity in speaking and interacting is more often evident.

My current spiritual practices contain elements from the Headless Way, Vipassana meditation, and Ramana Maharshi's self-enquiry, among other sources. Seeing what's here can be practised in whatever situation in one's daily life: working, washing dishes, driving, whatever, via the experiments or not, as an 'informal' practice. This can be complemented or reinforced with a regular period of traditional or 'formal' meditation practice of sitting or lying-down for twenty or thirty minutes to focus on who or what is seeing. It's similar to the usual Vipassana practice of being aware of the breath moment to moment, letting the habitual cloud of thoughts disperse in the clarity of awareness, or seeing. See the Capacity for the thoughts, where they come from, where they go, who or what is having them and aware of them. Who? There, or I should say here, the seeing goes on in its simple availability celebrating life's value and grace.

The Seeing, the breathing, the experiments, any reminder that I AM, whatever is at hand will suffice. It's sweet and sour to remember spending the first part of my life striving to build up a good head on my shoulders only to then shrug it off and leave it for others to take in or not, while I am taken with what was all along really here, barefaced, unforeseen, astonishing, yet feeling like home.

Bill

Practical headlessness - the other day I was sitting, solidly, in a dentist's chair (it's the patient's chair after all, isn't it?), while two people occupied themselves with the usual poking, prodding and stuffing of sucking, wheezing, whirring, and boring instruments into my mouth. Not exactly fun, but then I recalled that I didn't have to perceive it all that way, and gave it up. Then there were just these two odd people sticking their hands and all that gear into some void on my lower horizon, apparently, and with a near comical seriousness of purpose (although thank God for that!).

Thomas

I encountered *On Having No Head* purely accidentally while on a kind of retreat in the mountains. I saw the point of some of the exercises, but still felt that there had to be more. This was in 1988. In 1989 I was consumed with the question of Who Dies? The problem was I knew the answers intellectually; perhaps even had a feel for what was being pointed to, but death and its fears still consumed me. In 1993 I re-read *The Little Book of Life and Death*, and BANG! How silly, no one to die!

Kriben

'Down, in, through' seems to work. In the beginning I thought seeing would solve my problems. In the end I realised 'When all else fails, seeing is what's left.' As long as we exist as a mind-body we are obliged to do what we can as such. But it is immensely reassuring to know that in the bigger context of 'what we really are', we are OK and cannot fail.

Colin

———————————

I just want to tell you that this evening I shared seeing with a friend through the 'card experiment'. Although I tried to share it with her before (using the pointing and tunnel experiments), it did not work; but tonight she really had the 'implosion'. How nice it is to share this seeing with others. The greatest gift one can receive, and the greatest one to give to anyone.

Jan

INTERVIEWS

Interview with Douglas Harding, 1977

Richard: Is your message something new in the world?

Douglas: No, and yes. Far from being new-fangled, it's deeply traditional. After all, it's just another version of the Perennial Philosophy that's been around for perhaps three thousand years. The basic doctrine of the Perennial Philosophy is that you and I are God herself travelling incognito. The one we all really are is the one reality behind all things – call it God, Buddha-nature, Atman-Brahman, what you like. What one is doing is only to connect up with and celebrate and live from this perennial wisdom, which is to be found at the very heart of all the great religions. There it is, unrecognised, neglected, scorned, denied, but there it is. One is simply continuing in this tradition as best one can. That's the first part of the answer. The second part is: yes, there is something new here and I think it has to be new if it is to be alive. I think that every real enjoyer of this superb, supreme essential insight comes to it from a different place. Every real discovery of this is through a unique gate, and this gate of mine is not going to be exactly like anyone else's. In fact it happens to be different – a real breakthrough – and in some quite important respects. It's a thoroughly contemporary approach with its own new and very effective technology, and its procedure, which we call workshops. It seems to me that if it weren't up-to-date in this way it would be in danger of lapsing into a moribund, half-dead or altogether dead traditionalism. It tells the old old story, but in a drastically demythologised version. It is credible, now it is shorn of incredible embellishments. I would say that here we have demythologising at its limit at this time in history. Here the Perennial Philosophy is clarified and simplified, pared down to essentials – thanks to the experiments which are the heart of the matter.

Interview with Douglas Harding, 1983

Richard: You have been writing and giving workshops for many years. What is your work about?

Douglas: That's a question I need always to be asking myself. Not to have a pre-packaged, predetermined idea of what it is, but to address myself to it afresh every time. For this interview, Richard, I need to ask myself what I'm up to, all over again. What am I up to? Well, I'm getting pretty near the end of my life, and it would seem a very natural and proper thing to ask what was it all about, what was it for? Even more personally: what was it to live, what is it to exist? One of the first things I should say is that I find it a most extraordinary thing to exist, to have happened. I don't mean just to be Douglas Harding, but to be at all, to be aware, to be an awareness, or even Awareness itself. What an extraordinary thing and what a pity to come by this awareness, to be aware, and then not to get the taste of it! It seems an awful thing, sad and chicken-hearted and miserable, not to be interested in these matters. So, what I'm up to, at its briefest, is to wake up to the mystery of myself.

Richard: As well as your work on yourself, what about your work in the world?

Douglas: I see my work in the world as quite subordinate to my work on myself. I think that to have an idea that I can help, and exert an influence, or have anything of value for the world, is secondary to and dependent upon my having answered the basic question of what my own life is about for me. It seems I have nothing to tell other people until I have got my own act together and my own problem answered. But when I have done that, when I have awakened to what it is to be me - why then, since I find the simple truth to be so very different from everything I had conceived, so very much more valuable, so interesting, so marvellous, such fun, so profoundly affecting the way I live, how natural it is to want to share that with the world. As to the method of sharing it, I guess that will come out later in your questions.

Richard: What is the method?

Douglas: The method is the turning of attention through an angle of precisely 180 degrees. Our attention is normally directed outwards, ahead of us. It's directed at an object, and that's very proper. I'm looking at you now, my attention is Richard-wards, but at this moment where is that attention coming from? What is this arrow of my attention, what bow is it being shot from? What I do now is to turn the arrow round and notice that here is nothing like whatever I find there. So what I'm doing is looking in two directions, and they are diametrically opposite to one another. One is to look at what I'm looking at, which is Richard there, with one hand on his chin and a pen in the other, looking at me. In the other direction, at an angle of 180 degrees to that picture of Richard, is the absence of anything like that. I just find absolutely nothing here. Certainly nothing corresponding to what I find there. Here is no face, no head to confront Richard with. I find myself emptied in his favour, and this is the essential experience from which all proceeds. This emptiness-for-others is what I'm enjoying, and when I try to share it with people, and bring it out into the world, this is the thing I get them to look at, each for himself or herself. I can't tell them what to find, but I can encourage them by telling them what I find. I want people to check whether they are in the same condition as I am, or not.

Richard: So you are seeing that for yourself you are different from what you look like.

Douglas: To be a 'normal' human being is to be conned into the proposition that I am what I look like. Well, I say I'm not what I look like. More, I'm the opposite of what I look like. When I say look like, I mean look like to you over there.

Richard: You look like a man to me.

Douglas: Of course I look like a man to you at six feet. But I'm looking at myself at zero feet and I can't find any of those features you are in receipt of. Here are no eyes, no mouth, no cheeks, no beard. So I find that we are not, Richard, at this moment, face to face. I've never in all my life been face to face with anyone. It seems to me this face-to-face thing is a great hoodwink, the universal confidence trick which I'm sure, in the end, will be ruinous for living, for many reasons.

Richard: How did you come to this realisation?

Douglas: I think just from living such a messed-up life, from being so unsatisfactory a person: I just had to find out what had gone wrong. Plus having, perhaps, more than my fair share of curiosity and inquisitiveness, so that eventually I just had to look at myself for myself. Having read and thought and cogitated about this question of my identity for ages, I found myself simply looking to see, and daring to be my own authority on the only place that I am in a position to pronounce on. Nobody else can tell me about it, about what I'm like right here being me now, coincident with myself. Once I had asked myself what I was looking out of, it became instantly apparent that it was the exact opposite in every way of what I had been told. To get face to face with you now, I have to hallucinate something here to match what I see there on top of your shoulders. It seems to me, Richard, that to live my life on the basis of a central lie is a rotten life, as an apple with a rotten core is a rotten apple.

Richard: How does this awareness of who you are, that you are not a thing in the world - affect your life? How do you think it might affect other people's lives?

Douglas: In so many ways. I can only just begin to speak of them. Nothing is unchanged. I have difficulty in knowing where to begin, but I'll begin, in a way, at the end. This new awareness means that when I look in the mirror I look at something which has got a terminal disease, namely life. That one in the mirror is living, that one was born, that one is going to die. That one is changing all the time. And it's not at all what I am. It's what I appear to be. It's not my central reality. It is one of my appearances, and is dying. What I am here is in total contrast to that, because here is nothing to change, let alone die. It's obvious that all things, from galaxies to particles, perish. So if I am a thing I am perishable. All my appearances are things, are phenomena, but the reality from which they proceed is not a phenomenon, is not a thing. It is awareness of itself as free from thinghood.

Richard: What about our interaction with people, animals, even things?

Douglas: A symmetrical relationship, person to person and face to face and thing to thing, has got to be the opposite of, absolutely different from, a 'relationship' (it's not a relationship at all) between no-thing and things. My 'relationship' with everything imaginable, every person, is totally and absolutely asymmetrical. Which means in practice that instead of relating to that person, I am that person. I am him or her in the sense that that is my appearance at this time, that is the guise I am wearing. It's the form I am taking at this moment. You at the moment are forming, shaping me. It's as if I'm Richard-ed. That is a marvellous start because it means I am not opposed to you, I am not confronting you, not up against you. Confrontation is our trouble, it is what our world suffers from. The consequence of seeing who I am is finding that I cannot, will not, ever, confront anything in my life. Confrontation is out. Confrontation is the clash of two similar objects. Confrontation is the great lie on which our lives and society are based. Get rid of that lie and try out what happens. It means universal love.

Richard: This revolution in personal relationships must have an effect on one's relationship with foreigners, animals and plants, inanimate objects - you name it. I'm thinking of all the conflict going on in the world today at all levels, and how you might help.

Douglas: I think that if we try to ameliorate, or abolish even, the dreadful things that are going on in the world - war and exploitation, starvation, pollution, all those things - if we try to do that at the level of the symptoms we're not going to do very much. I wouldn't say it's useless, but it's going to be insufficiently radical. We will not make a real contribution here until we tackle the root of the thing, and the root of the thing is to be found in each of our personal lives. If I'm suffering from this disease of confrontation in my relationship with you at this moment, what's the use of trying to deal with the same problem of confrontation at other levels - national and international - between sexes, ethnic groups, religions, ideologies, power blocs, and so on? In other words, service to the world begins at home. Repeat: service to the world begins at home - if only because when you've found out who you are you find you are the world.

Richard: How do you think this discovery affects such psychological problems as depression, anxiety, fear and loneliness?

Douglas: There's a sense in which it leaves those human things to carry on at their own level. At the centre of my life is this Awareness whose very nature I find is freedom - freedom not only from thinghood but from thoughts and feelings of all kinds. Certainly from problems of all kinds. As the source of those things, the origin of those difficult things, its business must be to leave them alone, free to be what they are. Who I really am doesn't in itself change what I like to call my human nature. What it does, Richard, is to place it. This difficult and sometimes heart-rending stuff is not denied. In fact it is far more honestly reckoned with and cheerfully taken on board, from the state of freedom at the centre, than ever it was from that illusory person. Now there's no necessity to deny and every reason to acknowledge these troubles in so far as they persist. Part of the price of involvement in the world is having these feelings, some of which are agreeable, some of which are disagreeable, some of which are tragic. I can't exist, can't express at all, without this dualism out there. The dualism of good and evil, beauty and ugliness, black and white, etc. is the inescapable condition of expressing into the world from the place that is free of those dualities. So it's not a case of being free from these things, in the sense that one abolishes them, but of being free from them in the sense that one locates them. They are no longer central. This awareness not only removes one from them - without removing oneself from them - but in the long run, and when persisted in, changes them. How exactly this happens remains to be seen.

Richard: Do you find in your own life that you have arrived at a sense of deep peace through this awareness?

Douglas: Yes, I do indeed. It couldn't be deeper. It couldn't be more available, and it couldn't be more natural or native to us. It's been here all the while, and can never be achieved, or improved upon, or cultivated. It simply is here for the looking at. This peace is our very nature, not something we come across. It's where we are, nearer than all else. We don't come to it, we come from it. To find it is to allow ourselves to go back to the place we never left.

Richard: Can you say something about your 'new technology', the experiments?

Douglas: I've already described one of them – the one that perhaps is the best of all. When you have a face in front of you, the question you put to yourself is: 'Is anything here to match that?' I'm looking at your eyes now and I see two little 'windows', which you're alleged to be peeking out of. Rather marvellously! But I find here where I am no eyes at all, and certainly not two of them. Here I find just an enormous 'window', wider than east is from west. It has no frame. It's a kind of oval, yet of infinite extent. Instead of a pair of little peepholes here, this is what I find. Again, I look at the colour of your face now – how can I take in that colour if there is any colour here? I see the complexity of your beard, your hair, your pores, all those subtle variations of form and texture, and I note the total absence of everything from here. There I find a wonderful essay in complexity, here I find a wonderful essay in simplicity, total clarity, total freedom, total relief from what I find there. I find your eyes are moving. I find no movement here. When you walk down the passage, why that's what you do. But I find that when I walk down the passage I don't walk down the passage at all, the passage walks down me! If I go out in my car the whole countryside is moving! In fact everything in life, absolutely every part of life, is for me an opportunity for discovering that everything I had been told about myself – myself as I really am, right here – is upside down. It's incredible fun, as well as enormously important psychologically and spiritually, to tell the truth about oneself to oneself. Self-deception is both dull, and sick.

Richard: How do you see your future and the future of your work?

Douglas: I'll begin with the second one. What's going to happen to these techniques that I've just given some indication of? If the human race is going to survive (and it seems to me it has a fair chance of doing so), I think it will be because the experience of non-confrontation is spreading. The hope of the human race lies in this, and in similar, parallel ways of arriving at the truth of non-confrontation. It seems to me that we have come through a period in which this myth of confrontation, after an innings of perhaps a million years, has now become so counter-productive that it threatens our very survival. Our need is to discover that it is a myth, and to start living that other kind of life, the life of non-confrontation – in which each of us is emptied for the others. I see the future of my work as the continued pointing to the truth of non-confrontation and its necessity. I think that if it is a truth – and it is – it will look after itself. I think it's already becoming built-in in a kind of underground way, in a not too obvious way. This is not something which catches people by the throat. It's something that is working at a different and deeper level. The fact that already we're living from this truth is the guarantee of its survival. It's the way we are. It's not an achievement, it's a realisation – *the* realisation. Confrontation is a myth. The truth can be trusted to look after itself. Therefore I have no worries about the future.

Interview with Richard Lang, August 2002

This interview was conducted by Laurent Grégoire during a week-long workshop I led at Le Taillé, a retreat centre in France.

Laurent: Richard, in what circumstances did you first hear about the headless way and how did this discovery affect you?

Richard: I was seventeen and still a schoolboy. I had become an active Christian when I was twelve or thirteen, but I was particularly interested in mysticism. I wanted to see God! When I reached fifteen or sixteen it became clear to me that the Christians I knew were more interested in doing good than in seeing God. Doing good is marvellous. I am not criticising it, but I wasn't finding through Christianity what I was looking for. This was the late sixties.

So I put Christianity aside and began investigating other faiths – and wrote an article about each of the great religions for the school magazine. In my studies I came across Buddhism, and in one book found an advert for the London Buddhist Society summer school. I decided to go for four days - about half its duration. My twin brother David went with me. We travelled by train from Yorkshire to the summer school in Hertfordshire. I was a shy young boy and it was a strange situation to find myself in. I didn't know much about Buddhism. I was hoping to get enlightened I suppose! I remember there were meditation sessions with a Japanese Zen master – a very stern looking man. I was so shy and naive, I didn't dare go in.

In those days I was often in a daydream. Someone would say something and I wouldn't hear. Then one afternoon at the summer school I attended an informal workshop with Douglas Harding – it wasn't on the programme. I think Douglas didn't give a formal talk that year. Instead a friend of his, Colin Oliver, spoke, but he had already done so by the time David and I arrived. I don't know why we went to the workshop. I suppose we were talking to people and someone recommended it. So David and I stumbled into this workshop probably knowing little, if anything, about it. There were ten or fifteen people there and we did some of the experiments. I remember we did the pointing, but I'm not sure if we did the tube. I don't think the card experiment had been invented at that point. Instead we moved our hands back into the void. We didn't do the no-head circle because that hadn't been invented either.

David and I got the point, so we stumbled out of this workshop without our heads! Although we got the point and could see its value, we had a problem with Seeing, because Douglas at the time was talking about looking at people and finding no consciousness there, in people's heads. The only consciousness was where you were - in your no-head. David and I got the impression that this made people into something like cardboard cutouts, with no consciousness. We could see what he was talking about, but we felt concerned. Didn't this diminish the value of people by making them into unconscious objects? Wasn't this a dangerous attitude to cultivate? But fortunately we had Douglas there with us, so we were able to talk through such doubts over the following day or two, and to sort things out.

After the summer school David and I went back home to Yorkshire. My mum had been worried about us – two seventeen year old boys going to this strange conference in the south of England. Buddhism was very new in England at this time, and it was probably associated in the popular mind with hippies and drugs. But she said later that she took one look at us when we arrived home and realised we were okay.

I went back to school after the holidays for one more term, after which I was going to take the rest of the year off before I went to Cambridge University the following autumn. I was reading Douglas's *On Having No Head* and I was talking about it with my school friends. Seeing had made a big impression on me. My mother realised that something important had happened to David and myself so she organised a visit to see Douglas. She wanted to meet this man who had so affected her sons.

We spent a weekend with Douglas at his home in Suffolk. It was an opportunity to talk at length with Douglas - to raise questions and voice doubts, and get some answers.

In January 1971 I went to America, on an exchange scholarship to a school in Virginia. I lent *On Having No Head* to a teacher there and the next day he came back to me with a huge smile on his face. He had got the point! After school I hitch-hiked round the States during the summer and shared Seeing with several people. I was eighteen.

I returned home to England and in October 1971 went to Cambridge. My brother David, during the previous year off, had hitch-hiked to India - as people did in those days. I remember getting a letter from him when I was in the States and finding we were thinking about similar aspects of Seeing. We were both trying to integrate or understand Seeing and fit it into our own experience and understanding of life.

At university I was studying history, but history was the last thing on my mind. I was interested in Seeing, which seemed the total opposite to studying the past. Of course, it's not, but that's how it seemed at the time. I am grateful for my three years in Cambridge. As a history student there you are left very much to yourself, so I had lots of free time to devote to Seeing. They trust you to get on with your work. I used to spend my time walking round the town, watching the streets move, practising Seeing! I would find places that looked like the paper tube - college cloisters, avenues of trees. I would stand for ages at one end looking down the tube-like shape of the cloisters or the avenue, practising Seeing, being the space here at the near end. I would watch people, very small in the distance, get bigger and bigger until they disappeared into me - into the space here. So it was a lot of fun, and it was a time of sustained practice. I really was determined to See.

By chance Cambridge was not far from Nacton, where Douglas lived. So I used to go down there at weekends - perhaps every other weekend, sometimes more. This was between 1971 and 1974. There was often a group of about fifteen people there. Douglas has two houses, one solely for people to come and stay in. He lived in the other house with his first wife, Beryl, who was not at all interested in Seeing, so he couldn't have friends staying there - except on unusual occasions. When we had visited with my mum she stayed there. Normally people stayed in the lower house - a lovely building with one huge window covering an entire wall, like the single eye. I think Douglas had designed it with that idea in mind.

My time at university was spent reading everything Douglas had written, going to his house, talking with him about Seeing, meeting new friends. There was excitement in the air. It was a creative time for myself and my friends because we realised we could play with Seeing. We could make up new experiments. It was fun. I was able to explore Seeing with a great deal of support from Douglas and others. Here was a group of friends all interested in Seeing. Often we would gather together at weekends for workshops. I knew, right from the beginning, that I wanted to be involved in the work – or the play – of sharing Seeing. It was just the way it was for me. I remember standing on a street corner in Cambridge on a summer's evening and seeing a student I vaguely knew walking towards me. I was being space for Cambridge, as the evening light gradually faded. He asked me what I was doing and I replied, 'Well, I'm being space for the people and the street.' I pointed out who he really was there and then. I think he walked away wondering what had hit him, or perhaps whether or not I was mad!

By the last year in Cambridge I was running a weekly workshop in my room. A friend of Douglas's, Jane, who worked in one of the colleges as a librarian, used to come. Often eight or nine people would turn up.

I was visiting Nacton frequently. Douglas began to ask me to introduce the experiments. I remember the first time he asked me to do this: 'Richard, after the coffee break could you lead the closed eye experiment?' I was nineteen or twenty, and I thought, 'God, what a responsibility!'

Around that time we made *The Toolkit for Testing the Incredible Hypothesis*. David and I had done a lot of work on it with Douglas. We made all the boxes by hand. We used to go down at weekends and during the week in the holidays. It was also a chance to spend time with Douglas. *The Toolkit* is a two-person workshop, which you go through with a friend. Towards the end there is a short closed-eye experiment. One person reads the questions to the other and then you change round. I remember I went and found *The Toolkit* during the coffee break and learned the questions. When we did the experiment Douglas thought I had done really well. But that is a way of learning, isn't it? First you copy something, then later on you do it in your own way.

I used to go to workshop after workshop, in part learning how to introduce the experiments. I was gradually gaining a deeper understanding of the experiments, of Douglas' ideas, of this direct way of sharing this truth. Then in my last year at university, in 1974, Douglas invited me to go to the States with him. It was a great honour for me, and gave me more experience in leading workshops.

I think of my time at Cambridge as a period when I learned to 'swim' with Seeing. I practised and practised so that it became more and more a part of my life. I read everything by Douglas that I could get my hands on. And I began to gather many Seeing friends.

In 1974 I finished university. I was twenty-one and didn't know what to do with my life. I had had enough of education and being told what to do. I had worked very, very hard at school, and then not so hard at Cambridge. I had made a number of Seeing friends, and when I left Cambridge about twelve of us found a large house in London. We were hippies, and we all shared Seeing. David lived there as well, and friends were always visiting. It was a headless house and we called it 'Nobody Home'. We used to run weekly Seeing workshops. We were all, in different ways, into Seeing. Douglas sometimes used to come and stay with us – with his hippie friends!

Laurent: I am wondering how practising headless Seeing was for you, because I get the feeling that most of the time it was playful, fun and easy, whereas my experience - and it seems to be most people's experience – is that we have to struggle to come back to Seeing, even though it is our natural state.

Richard: No, it wasn't always easy. I had all the problems any young man might have, and I now have all the problems most adults have. I struggled a lot, emotionally. I suppose what happened was that I was spending a lot of time with Douglas and talking with him, and he would keep saying, 'Well that's very normal Richard, that's what being Richard is, that's the nature of Richard - to have problems.' I remember sometimes being depressed and lonely at university and it wasn't fun at all. But I had Douglas saying to me, 'That's okay, Richard, just keep Seeing! Where's the depression? If you're depressed, look for your teeth... Nothing there, neither teeth nor depression! Depression there to the absence of depression here!'

Then, living in a house with twelve people, there were lots of problems, even though the people were Seeing. But fortunately Douglas and other friends kept pointing here, reminding me of two-way Seeing. So that's what I did. So, yes, sometimes life was – and is – really difficult.

Laurent: How do you usually describe or explain headlessness to someone who has never heard of it?

Richard: That's an interesting one. I think it's more fun not to have a preconceived idea but to meet the person and then see what happens. It's important to listen to where that person is coming from. Then sometimes I just say: 'Have you noticed you cannot see your face?', and I move my hands into their spaciousness to draw their attention to it. I tend to assume these days, I take it for granted, that people will have no problem at all seeing who they really are, absolutely none, because it's so simple. I think I got that from Douglas. In the beginning I used to think this was a really difficult thing to share, that somehow you've got to get the person to say 'Yes'. You've got to get them to understand. So you've already then created lots of problems, because obviously they are not going to respond to Seeing in the same way that you do. But Douglas just used to say: 'They can't not see it - it's so simple.' Which it is. So now I tend to show them and then assume they've got it, and then perhaps try and increase their confidence that they have it. And listen to their response. But I will do at least one or two experiments with them. It's no good just talking about it.

I notice these days when I'm doing a workshop, like this one here in France, I tend to introduce the subject by placing it in the context of Douglas's story. I describe how he came to see who he really was. In telling his story it is easy to introduce such ideas as 'What you are depends on where you are seen from', because that is what Douglas was thinking about when he discovered who he really was. But it depends on the person I am talking to. I shared Seeing with someone recently in South Africa, and I had the card with me, so we did the card experiment. You can't not see the card disappear into the void when you put it on!

Laurent: You have been practising headless Seeing for more than thirty years now. In what ways have you improved your ability to come back to this empty space that we naturally are? Would you say that some specific tools or situations help develop our ability to come back to our true nature? You already mentioned that Douglas was present for you. Alain Bayod talked this morning about the three necessary conditions for practising and for reaching our goal: a Teaching, a community of practising friends, and a Teacher. So could you tell us what has proved to be helpful to you.

Richard: Again, I can only speak about my own experience. I saw the point, and I recognised that this particular way was very effective and exciting and new, and way ahead of its time. There was nothing else like this happening on the spiritual scene. It was very, very exciting, and still is. For example, I read *The Hierarchy of Heaven and Earth* very early on. I think I was the first person to read the original version and it blew my mind. Over the next eight years I totally absorbed myself in Seeing. I visited Douglas frequently, did many, many workshops with him, and all my friends were Seeing friends - I was completely involved with it.

In 1977, after living in the house in London, I thought, What do I do with my life now? I want to share Seeing, but it's not a job. There isn't that much to do anyway – Douglas is doing everything that needs to be done. I wanted to make my life about Seeing, but I didn't know how to do that. Douglas used to quote

Milton to me: 'They also serve who only stand and wait.' Well, I was doing a lot of standing and waiting! So I went back to Cambridge, where I had friends, and got a job working with old people. Living in Cambridge also meant I was near Douglas. I thought, 'If he needs help, I can easily go down there.' But he didn't need help – not much anyway. He was always very happy to see me, of course – we'd become friends by then. I guess he was my friend, teacher, father figure, the whole lot rolled into one.

There was a Buddhist society in Cambridge, and one evening a meditation teacher called Dhiravamsa gave a talk there. Funnily enough, eight years before, when I first met Douglas at the London Buddhist Society summer school, Dhiravamsa had spoken there too. At that time he was a monk from Thailand, an assistant abbot, I think. Eight years later he had left the order, got married, and had brought psychotherapy into his retreats, as well as dance, Tai Chi and other things. After his talk in Cambridge I thought, That's interesting – I don't know what they do in the world of meditation and retreats. I'm very familiar with the Seeing world, but here is a different world. I think I'll go on a retreat and find out what they do.

Dhiravamsa was due to give a retreat shortly after his talk, in the new year in 1978, so I decided to attend it. It was short, about five days, and was held in the Fens, very flat country in East Anglia, much of it below sea level. So it's damp there in winter. Halfway through I nearly left, it was so painful for me. Not just physically but emotionally. We were in silence, there was lots of meditation but also dance and chanting and other things. I decided to leave one evening but couldn't because there were no buses! So I had to stay till the next day. I talked to Dhiravamsa that evening:

'Why do I need to stay here? I can see who I really am just as easily in Cambridge!'

'Well, you don't have to stay, but the retreat is a cleansing process.'

'But the void is already clean.'

'Yes, but what's in the void gets dirty. Meditation is the process of purifying the contents of awareness.'

He suggested I kept an open mind overnight, and see how I felt in the morning. (This is obviously my own rendition of that conversation, from memory.)

I was annoyed with him. I wanted to leave. I had made up my mind I wasn't going to stay, and he was suggesting I keep an open mind. I thought No! That means I might stay! No! I wanted to get away from the pain I was feeling. But I also thought, He's right. It is wiser to keep an open mind. Damn!

In the morning the sun was shining, I felt a little better, so I decided I'd stay for the morning. And, as these things sometimes happen, the retreat changed for the better, and I stayed till the end.

I had passed through my resistance and not run away - not because of any qualities in me but because there had been no buses! During the rest of that day things in me changed. My hearing, for example, became very clear. I remember hearing an owl hooting, so clearly. There was no distance, nothing in the way of the sound. Of course, I can hear now that there is no distance, but on the retreat I had a stunningly clear experience of this. I was experiencing the process of cleansing Dhiravamsa had been talking about. My sense of hearing, and seeing, had been purified - for the time being.

I found I was happy with sitting meditation – happy just to sit and be quiet. I was also happy with dancing. So when I got back to Cambridge I decided to explore this work more deeply. But I didn't want to go on retreats just now and then, when I could take time off work. I wanted to jump wholeheartedly into the experience. So a few months later, after saving some money by driving a van, I joined the community at the Buddhist Vipassana centre, Chapter House. The atmosphere was open and informal. There were no monks or nuns there, just ordinary people practising meditation. I had just enough money to stay for four months. I didn't know what I would do afterwards. Two months after I joined the community the assistant director recognised I was coming from a deep place and asked me to train to lead retreats. It seemed as though a door through to a magical country I had always wanted to travel in had suddenly opened. I said yes. I spent the whole of the next year training, which meant attending all the retreats at the centre. Dhiravamsa came over from the States (where he was then living) in the summer of 1979 and I did a long training with him – lots of meditation, bodywork and groupwork. For the next three years I lived at the centre and led ten day retreats, one after the other, plus many week-end retreats. This was a challenging and marvellous learning experience.

During this time I still kept in touch with Douglas. At one point I brought Douglas to the centre to run a weekend workshop, and often I would go and help Douglas with workshops elsewhere in England and abroad. But essentially I was now working at Chapter House, running retreats. The people there knew about headlessness through me, but they were not interested in it like I was. And Douglas and my Seeing friends were not interested in meditation. During this time I struggled, not quite knowing where I stood. I thought, headlessness is fantastic, it is really fantastic stuff, but this meditation is great too – but they are different paths. Douglas and his workshops are direct pointers home to the truth – far more direct than the teachings here at the centre. Yet they involve a lot of talk, whereas in the retreats there is silence! Silence is a relief for me. I can simply be quiet with the void! I can drop and drop, down into the abyss. In Seeing workshops you get the point simply and clearly, whereas there is often confusion at the centre, amongst people on retreat or in the community. They are not clearly awake to who they really are. Also, Seeing workshops are mostly sedentary, whereas in the retreats we also dance as well as sitting still. In Seeing workshops you do the experiments, yet there is often not much room to share or interact with others, but on retreat there is. And we sing and chant and do bodywork, and I like this. It is good for me. And a great deal of learning comes out of the groupwork at the centre.

Of course there are also many ways in which Seeing and meditation are similar. So I was in two camps, feeling pulled one way and then the other, and I was confused. Which path was my path?

I think Douglas was somewhat confused about what I was doing, or at least disappointed. 'What has Richard gone and done? He's off doing other things! Why does he need to do that?' (My words!) There was some tension there, the son leaving the father. But only on one level. Our friendship continued and deepened. But I was struggling. 'On the one hand is the headless way and on the other is the meditation way and I like them both. Which path is mine? Which group am I in?' It was only as I was leaving Chapter House, after four years there, that I realised, 'Richard, who you really are is not in either group! In as much as headlessness and meditation are forms, they are different in some ways and similar in others. But you don't have to choose between them. You are the space in which they both happen. Take from each what you want and leave what you don't want.' I had as a young man deeply absorbed the headless way and Douglas's ideas. Then I got deeply into the Buddhist path, giving it my all. Now it was time to relax into the spaciousness that belonged to neither and discover my own view out from this nothingness.

I left Chapter House in 1982, when I was twenty-nine. I remember saying to Tew Bunnag, the assistant director: 'I've finished all this training in retreat work, in running groups. It's been a fantastic experience, but it's not a qualification. I'm leaving here with no piece of paper. What use is this going to be in my life?'

He had a good response: 'It will come in useful, Richard. You will use your experience here. You can't see now how you'll use it, but you will.' He was a wise and good man. Dhiravamsa was the same. I saw him a couple of weekends ago in Spain where he now lives. We have a lovely friendship.

So I left Chapter House with not a clue about what I was going to do – and just with fifty pounds in my pocket. The centre paid me £7 a week, and during the last year this went up to £14 a week! But I got free board and lodging, and I received the training. The experience was priceless. There was no other way I could have got such an experience. It was unique and fantastic.

I then decided to visit my brother in California. So I went to London and worked for a couple of months as a waiter and earned enough money to go to the States. I stayed with David and his wife for three months, visiting various spiritual groups. I was checking out the spiritual scene there. This would be 1983, when I was thirty. But it didn't work out. With hardly any money left I had to return to England. I arrived back with no job, no place to stay, and with just £50 in my pocket – again!

I remember thinking, I don't know what I'm going to do. I know what I want to do – I want to share Seeing, but now it's not so simple. My life is now not just about sharing Seeing, it's also about facilitating groups, about integrating the experiments with other methods such as meditation and dance. I want to use these other tools as well, but I don't yet know how to do it. Of course, I was only going to find out how to integrate these things by working it out in practice.

Then by chance I met a friend in London who was training in psychotherapy.

At Chapter House someone had looked at the books in my room and commented, 'Richard, all your books are about meditation and spirituality. What about psychotherapy?' I didn't know much at all about therapy. Meeting this friend made me realise I needed to study psychotherapy. I didn't want to be a psychotherapist, but I wanted to find out what this very popular method of healing was all about. I had stumbled upon my next step. I thought, If I'm going to have credibility when I'm sharing Seeing, I need to be able to understand and speak the language of therapy since it's so popular. Otherwise I won't be able to relate to people's experience in this field. I had no money and it was necessary to put a deposit down for the training – I chose the one my friend was doing. So I got a job washing up and sent in my hundred pound deposit, just in time. Then I got a job working with children for three years and that financed my way through the training.

During the psychotherapy training I had to face the same issue that had come up at Chapter House – but now I was comparing headlessness with psychotherapy, as if I had to choose between them. Again, I was struggling with integrating new methods of awakening and healing with the ones I was already familiar with. It was a confusing time. And I was having to face uncomfortable aspects of myself that came into consciousness during the training, so I was also struggling psychologically. This had happened at Chapter House too.

I was now working out for myself how Seeing and therapy fitted together. These days I think of it in terms of two-way attention and two-way healing. In my mind and body there is an ongoing process of problems unfolding and, hopefully, being healed. But here [pointing to the centre where Seeing arises] there is always absolute health. There [pointing outwards] you are always changing. You resist and you let go, you resist and you let go. This will always be the case. I think we have all been experiencing this in one form or another during this week-long workshop here at Le Taillé. So meditation and therapy – and Seeing – have two aspects, two directions. The therapy here at centre is total therapy, total healing, whilst the therapy there, the healing there, in one's mind and body, is partial and gradual – just as the Seeing is total here but partial there. Two-way attention includes both sides. Both are important and both need attention.

Laurent: Do you consider your relationship with Douglas a teacher-student relationship or a guru-disciple relationship? I imagine he wouldn't consider it as either...

Richard: I can only speak for myself. I met him when I was seventeen and he pointed me home to who I really was. I was very young and he was obviously much older, he must have been about sixty then. He'll deny being a guru, but he also knows he is a guru. Anyway, my experience is that he showed me home, so I guess I can call him my teacher. I think of him like that. And there are the teachings, if you want to put it that way, that Alain was talking about, which came from Douglas and which fit with the teachings of other traditions. So I accept that too. Douglas's teachings are very clear. It is amazing to me because right from when he started, his teaching has always been basically the same. I think he worked it out through writing *The Hierarchy,* and through living it. The earliest articles are the same in essence as the ones he writes now. He's very consistent in that way. Of course, things have changed and developed. I also think his teachings are influenced by his Christian background. There is a deep Christian flavour to them.

So for me he was obviously an impressive person. I was a bit frightened of him to begin with, but what he said made sense to me and I began to put it into practice, so in that sense he was my teacher. He invited me, and anyone else interested in Seeing, to his house, as a friend. He did not set himself up above people. He was a friend, and he always said, 'You've got it now, exactly as I have. Now it is yours. You are doing it perfectly.' So he didn't set up any difference between himself and others. There was no hierarchy. I was very grateful for his teachings. He was always pointing me back to this place which is the same for us all. So I grew up with all that. Anyone who valued Seeing he called a 'friend' - a bit like the Quakers, I suppose. When anyone came to visit Douglas, lots of us would be there, and the point of being together was to share Seeing together. So I think of him as a teacher, yes, and as a friend, and as a father figure too. Just then in my life I think I was probably looking for someone to give me directions and Douglas was there. I don't think of him as my only teacher. For example, I also regard Dhiravamsa as a teacher and a friend - and a father figure I guess. There are other people too. I take on board what Douglas used to say, and still does, that everyone is your teacher. That is very interesting regarding the group here at Le Taillé, isn't it? Give people the opportunity to talk and they become your teacher and you find out something you didn't know, from their unique perspective.

I think it was a good model: the Friend, the Teaching and the Sangha [referring to Alain Bayod's talk]. There are many models, and we need models, we need frameworks, to a degree...

Laurent: After more than three decades of practice do you find there is a shift in your awareness, that you are spending more time seeing the obvious than thinking about yourself as a limited character known as Richard Lang?

Richard: I still think of myself as Richard, probably just as much as I ever did. That hasn't gone away. I have direct access to the Source, and I suppose in some ways the Seeing is more continuous. But saying that is almost meaningless, because the Source is not a thing in time. I think I just go on in my life yet keep returning here to the Source. Ever since I met Douglas I have taken that route and I'm doing it now. It is important to me. For some people it's not important to be awake to who they really are. It's important to me for lots of reasons - sometimes because I really need it, sometimes it's just a pleasure, sometimes it just happens, and sometimes simply because it's true. When I'm sharing Seeing I like to stress the fact that when you're home you're home for ever. It's timeless here. The Source is not a thing in time. I don't think very much about whether the Seeing is continuous or not. That doesn't really mean much to me.

Laurent: Over the years has Seeing got easier? Is there less resistance?

Richard: No, I don't think it's got easier. It's just the same – because it's still as totally available now as it always was, and because I think I'm just as resistant as ever. I don't think there is any difference really. Of course, things do change, I notice change, but I also continue to have problems. But, as I said, it's as available now as it was when I first saw it – because it's always been totally available. So, no, I'm afraid it hasn't got easier!

Laurent: Thank you for being so encouraging!

Alain Bayod: Douglas often says that only other people can say if you have really changed. You can't see it yourself.

Richard: I know there are some ways in which I have changed. My experience has changed, my view out. I have experiences now that I didn't have in the past. Life keeps evolving, keeps going deeper. For example, just before I came here I became more aware of how I take people's faces from them and they can't stop me doing it! I'm stealing their faces! In a sense I'm Seeing for them - I'm relieving them of their faces. I have their faces here in my no-face, and they don't have them. I had a deep feeling about this. I had never seen and felt quite like this before. So insights like that come through and then they go. Yes, I see changes, but I can't deny that I also experience my own personal difficulties and problems.

Another thing – when I'm leading groups these days, not just headless groups but psychotherapy groups, dance groups, any groups, I find I'm trusting the void to help me. I think it is complex because the more you go on doing something the more you can relax with it. You know you have the skills so you don't really have to prepare so much because you've done it so many times before. So there is that side to it. But the other side is recognising, through experience, that the void is smart, is intelligent, and that you can rely on it. You experiment with living and acting from 'not knowing', and you find that it works. So I think your trust deepens. And it's a lot more fun not knowing what is going to happen! So perhaps I take more risks as time goes on. Like now – I don't know what I'm going to say next! Of course, one never knows, but it's more interesting, more fun, when you are aware of it. And sometimes it's more scary... because you really don't know what is going to happen. I think surrender, if it is true surrender, is not an easy thing. It involves letting go when one doesn't want to let go. There is often suffering before there is peace.

Laurent: After so many years of practice and sharing, what is the most valuable contribution of headlessness to your everyday life?

Richard: Different things are valuable at different times, depending on what I need. If I'm feeling frightened of death then it's comforting to have access to the place where I don't die. Or if I'm missing someone I love and I'm feeling sad, then I'm comforted by seeing they are here in spirit where I am. Here we are one. If I'm experiencing a difficulty in a relationship with someone and I don't know what to do, then I have a resource I can draw on - I can relax back into this spacious not-knowing and wait and see what comes from it. I can wait for guidance. When I realise I can't work something out by myself, I can turn to this infinite resource within me. I can trust this One within me. If I am disappointed with myself then it is helpful to see my little self in the light of my spaciousness. I suppose I might say to myself, 'Well, God is in charge and God wanted this. You don't like this, you don't want it, but it seems God is deciding that this is what you've got to go through.' So I have a place I can wait in and trust.

Or if I am dancing - I used to find dancing so difficult because I was so self-conscious. Seeing is a fantastic thing! It's a secret isn't it! You're invisible and everyone is inside you. Dancing becomes fun! You let God dance your body and all the other bodies. You are room for the other dancers. Sometimes in the psychotherapy groups I lead, which are not overtly headless groups, I say that we heal one another. But this is what headlessness is about, isn't it? I am healed, my separation is healed, by my disappearance in favour of you.

I need profound experiences in my life. Such experiences are healthy. I need to plumb the rich depths of the world, and headlessness gives me a key. I don't know which depth it's going to take me to, but if I stay with Seeing it takes me to these depths and heights, which I then have to let go of. So headlessness is helpful with giving me the deep experiences I need, and helpful in allowing me let go of them when I need to.

Seeing is a fantastic thing to share with friends, it's a great thing to have in common. When I speak on the phone with my friend Carl in the States – I've never met him, but he got the point of Seeing from the website – we talk about looking out of the same big Window. That's amazing, it's so intimate. We can both see our phones disappearing into the void, we can hear our two voices coming and going in one Silence. It's mysterious and wonderful - and fun. We have different views from this big Window, but the Window itself seems to be the same. When we talk on the phone we laugh a great deal. And we are astonished at this miracle of being. You see the world so clearly sometimes, when you are Seeing. A veil is taken away and the world is beautiful.

Seeing is so practical too. If I am travelling somewhere, because I'm obviously not going anywhere, places are coming to me. So I can relax. Or when I'm writing, I know - I can see - this place that is infinitely creative... this bottomless abyss from which my thoughts emerge. See, and see what comes out!

Sometimes Seeing enables me to forgive myself, eventually. Sometimes I don't like myself at all. I get very disappointed. But with Seeing I can see myself from this spaciousness and somehow it is easier to accept myself as I am. Recently, in a very old friendship I made a mistake, I did something wrong. I didn't mean to but I did. To begin with I found it difficult to admit to this, but eventually I did. It was helpful to be not only Richard but also This. Seeing helped me hold my hands up and say, 'Yes, I was wrong.'

Laurent: Douglas sometimes compares Seeing to an infectious virus that is spreading. How do you view the coming years in terms of the possible development of this headless Seeing?

Richard: I'm very excited by the future. Who knows what will happen? I like to think of it positively, because if you're imagining it you're half-way to making it happen. So I'm manipulative...

Well, it may not happen - Seeing may not become recognised globally. But in my estimation the Seeing experiments really are a breakthrough. They are something new and exciting and effective and direct, and they work. People easily get the point from the website or from a friend - because of the experiments. Seeing is being passed around all the time. It's like a fire spreading. It cannot be stopped. I don't know how you could stop it. The nature of this fire is that it wants to spread. This is also a paradox, for when you see who you really are it's clear you're not seeing who you are as an individual. The One within all beings is waking up - to Itself. In that moment the goal is achieved, everywhere, for all time. So in this sense the journey is over, the job is done. It is also, at the same time, not done, the journey is not over. But when you stand in a crowded station, for example, and you see who you really are, you are seeing for and as everyone there - in fact, for everyone on the planet. They have no power to stop you!

You can't talk people's heads off, but you can love them off. It is a silent thing. You are loving everyone's head off and that's it. You are doing it for them without their knowing. This is very encouraging. You have the best of all worlds.

I think each of us is given something to do in life, whether it is to do with headlessness or not . Every so often, if I don't know what my next step is, I like to ask God, 'What do I do next?' Probably I already know what I have to do, but I'm resisting it, hoping He will give me something else to do! But He says 'Now you've got to write this, or make that video, or do the washing up, or make that phone call.' Then you can no longer deny that thing – yet how we sometimes resist!

Yes, something marvellous is happening. Seeing is growing in the world. But I don't think God really knows what is happening or what is going to happen. That's my impression. I will speak for God now...!

I'm amazed how things come out of nothing. I don't understand it. I cannot figure that one out. That's what life is like when you attend. Things are always happening, emerging out of nothing in a totally unpredictable way. Well, they are not totally unpredictable, but in detail they are. I think God enjoys that. I enjoy it.

Laurent: Did you have the opportunity to share this particular way of Seeing our true nature with students of spiritual traditions such as Christians, Islam or Buddhism? What kind of feedback did you get?

Richard: During the training at Chapter House, Dhiravamsa, who knew of Douglas but had not done a workshop with him, asked me to do the experiments with everyone on a retreat - perhaps twenty-five to thirty people. To me it is the same as sharing Seeing with anyone else. Everyone comes with his or her own unique view from the big Window. I've learned to relax more when I am sharing Seeing because I recognise that everyone's response is different. I used to want them to have a response like mine. Now I'm less bothered. In fact, it's more interesting if they don't respond in the same way I do.

Dhiravamsa once said to me: 'Don't get attached to the void, Richard.' And

I thought, Oh that's good, because the void is an idea, isn't it?

I'm happy to share Seeing with anyone. I have explored more than one tradition in some depth, and I like to find out where people are coming from, to understand their unique point of view. I have experienced being deeply involved with and attached to one spiritual path - headlessness - and then finding other ways to be useful. I have had to work out for myself how to relate to different ways home to who we really are, finding value in this or that method whilst remaining in touch with the freedom that belongs to no particular way. The freedom of our true nature. So it is interesting for me to share Seeing with people from different traditions and see how they begin to integrate it with their own path and their own way of seeing the world.

If I'm invited to share headlessness, in a workshop or one to one, then I feel completely free to use the experiments and the language of the headless way, and then people simply make up their own mind about it. The headless way naturally has its limitations. But the experiments are new and powerful. It is also exciting because there are so many ways in which they can be extended and developed.

Alain Bayod: Have you ever talked with Douglas about what happens after Douglas?

Richard: When he dies?

Alain Bayod: Yes. In the sense of spreading the teachings.

Richard: Headlessness will in the end get corrupted just like every other human endeavour!

Alain Bayod: Generally we know that when a man who has started a method dies, a lot of things happen.

Richard: I think, for me, I'll just continue doing my own thing...

Alain: Yes, but your thing is in exactly the same line.

Richard: Years ago I used to wait around, hoping Douglas would give me things to do, and sometimes he did. But now I no longer wait for Douglas to ask. I'm getting on doing things by myself – with God's help! And I will continue to do this, even after Douglas has died.

Jean-Marc Thiabaud: You mentioned that as a teenager you were interested in mystical Christianity. Are you in contact now with people interested in this tradition?

Richard: No. It was Douglas who introduced me to the writings of the great mystics. As you know he is very deeply versed in those writings – as if he knows these people, and in some sense he does, through reading their works. I have heard a lot about them through Douglas, and read a lot too. I've enjoyed being inspired by these people, and not just from those in the Christian tradition.

Laurent: You mentioned *The Toolkit*. Is it still available?

Richard: No. We only made a hundred copies – in 1972 – and it would be difficult, and expensive, to reproduce it now. It's very complicated and some of it is in a sense out of date, in terms of how things are presented. It was a child of the times really.

I think it would be very interesting to do something interactive on a DVD-ROM or on the web. *The Toolkit* was a fantastic thing, but nowadays the medium is the computer. We just need someone who's got the money to fund such a project.

Laurent: Thank you.

Interview with Douglas Harding, 1977

Richard: Do you see Who you are all the time?

Douglas: Good question. Yes and no. Seeing Who one is occurs out of time because seeing Who one is is God seeing Who He is and God doesn't see from half past three until quarter to four. God sees out of time and one's seeing is not Douglas seeing that he is really God, it is God seeing that He is really God. It is out of time and so in that sense one doesn't see all the time or for some of the time, or in time. One sees out of time. Yet there is another sense of course in which one can say that one's seeing is more continuous. That is the common-sense way of talking about it, and we speak of people who flash into their Emptiness and then forget it, for months and months, and then meet a seer, or someone, and flash in again. There is a sense in which this does happen. It is a provisional way of speaking. Even for such people it is really out of time.

Richard: In talking about it in that provisional way, isn't there a danger in pronouncing that some see longer than others, or more continuously?

Douglas: I think there is no escaping the obvious fact that some are better at seeing than others. There are some for whom it is their life and there are some for whom it is an occasional click or glimpse. To go back to your question: Do I see all the time? I think this is very well answered by Ramana Maharshi. Somebody asked him if he saw all the time Who he was. He said yes, only sometimes it is not at the forefront of consciousness but is like the bass accompaniment in music, which you hear but don't attend to: you would certainly notice if it stopped. I would say my own case is rather like that.

Richard: Might you say that at some times you are more clear than at other times?

Douglas: No, I wouldn't put it quite like that. I would say the Clarity at some times is more attentive to itself, and at other times less so, and the emphasis is rather on what the Clarity contains.

Richard: Is seeing Who you are the same for everyone who does it, or does it admit of degrees?

Douglas: No, it can't. If it had content it could admit of degrees, but since it has no content, since it is the awareness of No-thing at all, there is no scope for variation while it lasts. How long it lasts, its steadiness or continuity, varies greatly, of course.

Richard: If there is nothing here how can you say that the void is 'real'? Surely there is only the world which comes and goes. There is just the world – no void. To speak of it is to make a thing of it.

Douglas: For a number of reasons I can say that it is Reality itself. I have already touched on one or two of them. This Void is not mere emptiness, it is not mere absence, it is Self-Aware. It is Self-Awareness itself, and that makes it quite different from a void which is just an unconscious absence. Secondly, as I said, it is full to overflowing, full of what it's entertaining. Thirdly, it says to itself, 'This is for real. I am this. I AM.' It has its own interior self-justification. It is self-validating from within and when experienced cannot be doubted. It is after all what I'm most sure of, because I am it. All else is mere hearsay, is off centre, remote, changing, inscrutable, a product of ignorance. This Clarity I know because I am it. Here I have inside information, and only here. All the rest is external acquaintance. For all these good reasons I say it is real and all else is comparatively unreal.

BIBLIOGRAPHY

Douglas Harding titles published by The Shollond Trust:

Religions of the World: A Handbook for the Open-Minded
Look For Yourself: The Science and Art of Self-Realization
The Hierarchy of Heaven and Earth: A new Diagram of Man in the Universe
Head Off Stress: Beyond the Bottom Line
On Having No Head: Zen and the Rediscovery of the Obvious
The Little Book of Life and Death
The Science of the First Person: Its Principles, Practice and Potential
The Trial of the Man Who Said He Was God
The Spectre in the Lake
Visible Gods

Other publications:

Douglas Harding, *Face to No-Face: Rediscovering Our Original Nature*, edited by David Lang, Inner Directions
Douglas Harding, *To Be and Not To Be, That is the Answer: Unique Experiments for Tapping Our Infinite Resources*, Watkins
Open To The Source. Selected Teachings of Douglas E. Harding, edited by Richard Lang, Inner Directions

To find out more about this Seeing path, contact:

Richard Lang
The Shollond Trust
87B Cazenove Road
London N16 6BB
England
++44 (0)20 8806 3710
headexchange@gn.apc.org
www.headless.org

Printed in the USA
CPSIA information can be obtained
at www.ICGtesting.com
LVHW092119030124
767896LV00007B/315

9 780955 451263